The Mystery of
LOVE & MARRIAGE

Father George

St. Mary Press

P.O. Box 530681
Livonia, Michigan 48153-0681
www.stmarypress.com
Phone: 734-743-1041
Email: contact@stmarypress.com

The Mystery of Love & Marriage
by Father George H. Shalhoub

First Printing – August 2013
ISBN: 978-1-60047-890-1

Library of Congress Control Number: 2013944796
Interior photographs courtesy of Dreamstime.com

Scripture taken from the King James Version unless otherwise noted.

Scripture taken from the New King James Version®. Copyright © 1982 by Thomas Nelson, Inc. Used by permission. All rights reserved.

Printed in the U.S.A.

0   1   2   3   4   5   6   7   8

ACKNOWLEDGMENTS

I wish to state, from the outset, that I do not have the answers to life's mysteries. The mystery of love and marriage cannot be learned or discovered in a book. Rather, this mystery will unfold before your eyes, and the pages and chapters will become clear as we face the crises that come with love and marriage on a daily basis. Endurance and faithfulness make us not only assured of the future but also aware that we are not alone to face the future. Becoming a master of a relationship, even a disastrous one, is the combination of what we have inherited from our parents, family, friends, colleagues, and anyone who has inspired us on the road of life.

This book could not be the work of one individual, but a community of participants. I wish to express my deep gratitude to those who traveled the uncharted road and taught me what makes a husband, a dad, a friend, a pastor, and a teacher, for no man is an island and no one author has all the answers. But every author brings the excellence and expertise of others and embraces it as they offer it to their readers.

I wish to acknowledge, with a debt of gratitude, first, my own family, our greater family the Church, the community in Livonia, and colleagues whether in the ministry or education. And at St. John of Damascus School of Theology: Philip Abdelhaq, D. Khoury, S. Haddad, E. Bitar, J. Zihlawi, G. Sabbagh, J. Shalhoub, and M. Najim, and especially Dr. Bess Kypros with whom I have taught the marriage and family course at Madonna University, and Sister Rose, PhD, dean of

Madonna University. Thanks to my childhood and adult professors, my colleagues at the Antiochian House of Studies, and its dean, Dr. Joseph Allen, to my co-workers Jim King, Mary Rice, Issa Rizkallah, and Dennis Bojrab, MD, and to my most dedicated secretary, Stacey Badeen. I would like to acknowledge also Y. Zakhour and B. Horani; many thanks to each of you.

Thank you to the generosity of individuals who read my first draft of the manuscript and gave suggestions: Dr. Joseph Allen, Anthony Hughes, Anthony Michaels, and Dr. John Morgan who contributed the foreword. I owe a debt of gratitude to the late John Estephan, the late Ellis Khouri, and the late Michael Shaheen, all who molded my life with passion and perseverance, to J. Rahal, Anthony Gabriel, and C. Nasr, and to His Eminence Metropolitan PHILIP who exerted the greatest influence of excellence.

And last, but not least, thank you to my wife Nouhad and children Lila Zogaib-Lippert (Jason) and Cameron Lippert II, Drs. Alex and Melissa Shalhoub, Marc and Alexa Nassif, and Christa Shalhoub; and our grandchildren Andrew and Addison Zogaib, Cameron Lippert III, Olivia and Amira Shalhoub, and Sophia Nassif.

Father George

FOREWORD

> "Marriage is a revelation and mystery.
> We see in it the complete transformation
> of a human being, the expansion of
> his personality, fresh vision, a new
> perception of life, and through it, a
> rebirth into the world in a new plenitude."
> Fr. Alexander Elchaninov
> *The Diary of a Russian Priest*

Mystery, not magic, is the essence of the love and marriage success story as told by Father George Shalhoub in this fascinating book. From "first impressions" to "embracing endurance," the binding ingredient in the ultimate human relationship of the marriage bond is that of love. The mystery of the enduring regard for each other, rather than some mere shallow talk of a "successful marriage," is the focal point of Father George's telling inquiry into the depths of human emotion converging in marriage. It is too easy to speak glibly of a successful marriage when what we want, where our heart's desire is, can be found only in the profoundly experienced regard for the mate to whom our enduring love is extended and from whom it is never withdrawn. From infantile self-love to mature other-love constitutes the maturing journey toward love and marriage. This journey toward love and marriage is not magical but is infused with an abiding sense of enriching mystery of the heart and mind linked in a quest for total fulfillment in the human relationship.

In a world fraught with uncertainty, with suspicion, fear, and distrust, there should be, there must be, and certainly there is a place where the individual can find a safe, loving, trusting relationship with another person. That place is in a marriage showered with other-love, with love for someone else, for one's partner and mate. It is not enough to establish a formal arrangement wherein the institution of marriage is the binding force between two people. In such a relationship, there is little difference between marriage and a corporate contract. In this provocative and insightful exploration of the depths of the marriage relationship bound up in the mystery of love, Father George has shown that the fulfilling human experience of encounter can be and should be realized in the ultimate expression of other-regard in a marriage based on mature love.

John H. Morgan, PhD, D. Sc., Psy. D.
Karl Mannheim Professor
History & Philosophy of the Social Sciences
Graduate Theological Foundation
Mishawaka, Indiana

TABLE OF CONTENTS

"We are not speaking of an ordinary priest, but one who is extraordinary in every sense. His deep spirituality, and yet one who is immersed in the realities of this world, have made him a passionate pastor and a most decent human being."

Antony Gabriel
Professor of Eastern Study

"Blessed is the priest who serves the Lord with dedication and perseverance. Blessed is the minister who has the love of God in him, for he bears God to his parishioners."

Dr. Michel Najim
Professor of Dogmatic Theology

The Mystery of
LOVE & MARRIAGE

INTRODUCTION

"Marriage is the key of moderation
and the harmony of desires, the
seal of a deep friendship."
Saint Gregory the Theologian

From the first wedding in the village of Cana in Galilee, as described in the second chapter of John, where Jesus performed His first public miracle—turning water into wine for the wedding guests—Christians the world over have celebrated the sacrament of marriage as an extension of the marriage of Christ, the bridegroom, with His bride, the Church. Newlyweds set sail on a sea of matrimony, not knowing where their ship will take them or what perils they will face along the way. If they remain true to their shared values, strong faith, and common goals to become the best they can be, they will face their difficulties and challenges with courage and, with God's grace, they will triumph.

It may seem to be an unrealistic portrait of marriage that, with God's blessing, we will weather the storms and arrive safely on a beach of bliss. This is not my intention; rather, it is to show that the sacrament of marriage (the mystery of love, Ephesians. 5:21-

32), as it was established in the New Testament, provides a blueprint for the kind of married life we all desire, one of mutual helpfulness and shared goals. To achieve the ultimate marriage, through good times and difficult times, is yet another matter.

Books about marriage abound. They present an abundance of ideas on how to succeed in marriage, how to know if your marriage will fail, and how to save a broken marriage. What does *The Mystery of Love & Marriage* have that the other books and manuals do not have? As an Orthodox priest for more than forty years, I offer my perspectives gleaned from counseling hundreds of young couples before marriage, advising them during difficulties in their married life, and celebrating their milestone anniversaries.

As a husband, also for more than forty years, I understand why some people refer to marriage as a battle and why others take a more positive view, doing good deeds together and loving their way through married life, oblivious of the battle scars others acquire along the way. Realistically, married life is both a battle and a triumph.

We start preparing ourselves for marriage the day we are born, because our birth sets us on the path and starts us on our mission in this life. Our first impressions come from our family, our parents and siblings (if there are some, either before or after our birth). Our familial first impressions help to define us, but I must caution that they need not totally define us, as we shall see in Chapter 1.

Eventually, as we expand beyond family, we form new impressions of those outside our family and extended family circle. We form friendships with our peers, experience the growing pains of puberty, and encounter our first infatuations (puppy love), which are important toward developing more mature love as we get older. In Chapter 2, we will look at puberty and puppy love and how both lead us further down the path toward marriage.

The importance of loving ourselves is critical to all of our adult relationships. If we cannot love ourselves, Erich Fromm said, we cannot love others. Chapter 3 offers a number of ways we can develop this love of self, which goes together with positive self-esteem.

Where would we be without friends? Some contend we would not want to live, even if we had everything else we wanted. In Chapter 4, we discuss the value of friends and how they serve as mirrors to ourselves and how they complete us in many ways.

Chapter 5 takes us from friendship to the serious side of love at the threshold of marriage. Sometimes a couple takes a giant leap from love to marriage, but it backfires. Even couples embarking on second or third marriages can miss the cues that spell trouble down the road. It is critical for the in-love couple to know what bodes well for their relationship in marriage as well as the warning signs at this stage of a relationship that may doom the marriage.

From the time they are little girls, women dream of their shining knight, his romantic proposal, their wedding day, and their new life together. Chapter 6 presents the positive side of proposals and pre-wedding preparations, but it also sheds light on the realities of marriage, the good prospects and those that predict challenges, even failure. It is better to know these things at this stage than after tying a knot that might be difficult to untie.

Whether or not you follow the church's protocol for your wedding liturgy or write your own vows, Chapter 7 offers some valuable advice on the subject and also addresses the importance of understanding the commitment you are about to make. For those readers who are already married, this might be a good time to review the sacrament you took to refresh your commitment to each other.

Everyone talks about pre-wedding jitters, and there are plenty of those, but how many are concerned about post-wedding adjustments? Chapter 8 covers this territory and all the anxiety that couples experience when they first start living together as husband and wife.

Statistics show that money is one of the principal causes of the breakdown of marriage. If individuals have difficulty managing their own financial matters, they can bring those problems into marriage. Both partners need to be totally honest before marriage about their finances, debts, plans to repay debts, and their outlook on building a sound financial future for their family after they marry. Chapter 9 tackles the problem of money and marriage.

No matter how much a couple is in love or how smoothly their transition is from being single to being married, sooner or later, a serious problem will arise that puts pressure on the young couple. Chapter 10 gives insights into how we can better handle life's pressures, especially in marriage.

Beyond the pressures that befall a married couple are conflicts that occasionally arise, simply because two people of the opposite sex are living closely together as one. Conflict resolution is vital to the health of a marriage. Chapter 11 examines ways that a couple can minimize conflict and resolve major disagreements (dare we say battles?) without rushing to divorce court.

Forgiveness is one of the cornerstones not only of the Christian faith but also of all relationships, and in particular, the marriage relationship. In Chapter 12, we discuss how to become forgiving toward those who hurt you, emotionally or physically, for your overall, long-range benefit.

Chapter 13 offers loving gestures that couples may adopt on a pick-and-choose basis to show their love for each other. Some ideas are serious; others are whimsical. Some will have a short-term effect; others will make a lasting impact. Acts of love, delivered randomly and frequently, will be more natural the more regularly we practice them.

In our final chapter, "Embracing Endurance," we celebrate married couples who have been blessed to live and love happily for many years. What ingredients did they bring to their relationship that have stood the test of time?

Ideally, we begin from the cradle, learn to love ourselves first, form friendships, define our life goals, fall in love, and enter marriage psychologically and spiritually equipped to handle the daily challenges of life shared closely with another. No two journeys are alike, yet for Christians all are linked in the common bond of the marriage sacrament. Those whom God has joined together, no man should separate (Matthew. 19:6).

1

FIRST IMPRESSIONS

"Train up a child in the way he should go:
And when he is old, he will not depart from it."
Proverbs 22:6

Imagine what it is like for a baby to absorb his first impressions: the sounds of laughter, a lilting lullaby, an angry argument, a chirping bird, the comfort of a gentle hug, a cuddly teddy bear, mother's milk. In the midst of these first impressions, all but one of which engenders a warm and fuzzy feeling, there is the sound of an angry argument. Babies take in the good and bad first impressions, and even though when they grow older, they may not remember those encounters before the age of two, they still impact their life. First impressions in the early years help to define each and every one of us.

As we grow out of infancy into the toddler stage and beyond, the impressions we have acquired linger and further define us. For some children, however, the impression of an unhappy home, an alcoholic father or an untidy mother need not—and do not always—define us even when we are still young.

Kenny's mother came from an impoverished life before she immigrated. She saved anything and everything, even after it had passed its usefulness. Her collections littered every room in the house, and no one ever dared touch them. Kenny grew to dislike the disarray that defined their home. After his older sister moved out, he took possession of her bedroom and, though still a child, he immediately transformed it into an oasis of tidiness with everything properly put away. As loving as his mother was, Kenny did not accept his first impression of her as a homemaker to define him.

From birth, we set out on a path that will take us in and out of relationships for the rest of our lives. We start with our parents and siblings, as well as our extended family.

> Our path is one of discovery—who we are, why we are here, what our mission is.

The biggest boost toward discovering who we are comes from God Himself who made us in His image and likeness out of His love for us. What more could we want? It would be great if it were that simple. For some, it may take a lifetime to know the origin of self; for others, it may take struggles, hardships, and great difficulties, often reaching rock bottom, to look up and find the answers that, in Christian understanding, have been there all along.

Those of us who have been blessed with parents who live by good values, deeply-rooted Christian ethics, and upstanding morals usually start off on the right foot. We learn the basic values early on so that when we grow and get to know people outside the family circle, we are prepared to interact properly, respect others and their property, tell the truth, act in a trustworthy manner, and as a result, enjoy the riches that relationships offer.

Does birth order matter?

Studies, scientific and otherwise, show that the order of birth has some determination in how you relate to others and how you handle relationship; how others see you and how you see yourself.

The first born child becomes the beneficiary of all that goes with announcing the arrival of a couple's first bundle of joy—a pastel-painted nursery, soft, cuddly toys, and adorable infant wear. In addition to the material perks of being the first-born, the child reaps the benefits of being the center of attention in an adult environment, being impressed by the indulgence of a doting grandfather or an attentive nanny, and receiving the undivided attention of parents, extended family, and close family friends until the next child arrives.

In a real sense, the first-born child is raised by trial and error. The parents, who do not receive a manual to guide them, may pass on their own fears and anxiety to the first born. In some cases, if one or both parents were first-born children, the fears that they pass on to their first-born child can leave lasting scars.

Irene was an only child who grew up in a strict adult environment. When she was twenty, she married a young man who worked in another state. Irene became pregnant soon after she was married, but tragedy soon struck when her young husband was killed in an automobile accident. Irene became bitter, and her bitterness was reflected in the way she raised her only child, a daughter named Sally. When she grew up, married, and had her first child, Sally unintentionally passed along some of the bitterness with which her mother had raised her. Irene doted on her young granddaughter in ways she had not shown Sally. The effects of these dysfunctional relationships lingered for many years, with Sally's daughter feeling unloved by her mother. Sally had three more children, and they grew up with closeness to their mother with which the eldest sister could not identify.

Beyond material adornments, first-born children have some advantages over subsequent siblings. The first-borns enjoy the praise and support when they speak their first words, take their first steps, even eat their first solid food. Whatever these children do earns rewards of some sort—a big smile, a "good girl" or "good boy" word of praise, or a gentle hug. These early accomplishments and support build their self-confidence.

Subsequent arrivals, regardless of the time gap between them, receive enthusiastic welcomes, but these children often become the recipients of "hand-me-downs" from earlier siblings. It is not quite the same treatment as the first-born receives. There are many generalizations about personality traits in children, depending on the order in which they were born. First-born children are good leaders; middle-born children are natural achievers, and last-born children are spoiled, garnering more attention as the babies in the family.

According to a theory proposed by psychiatrist Alfred Adler, the first-born child is "dethroned" when the next one arrives, and they may never recover from that. If not recognized and addressed, it can lead to serious complications in adult life.

One such example of dethroning is eight-year-old Molly. She seemed to be troubled and stand-offish in school. In art class, she didn't draw happy pictures in bright, cheerful colors like the other girls in her class. Instead, Molly's drawings were always of a big brown hill, a mountain of dirt, on which she drew three stick-like trees, two large ones, and one small one. She never varied either the dark colors or the three objects on the hill. One day, the teacher asked her about the meaning behind these repeated dark drawings. Molly bluntly blurted out that she liked her life better when she was the only child.

Did Molly's parents know that she resented being upstaged by her siblings? Had Molly's parents not prepared her to welcome more children into the family? Had her parents not considered the impact a new baby would have on Molly after being the only child for a few years? Perhaps they just assumed that she would enjoy having a baby brother or baby sister. Parents often take for granted their children's acceptance of something beyond their control.

In a parent-teacher conference, Molly's parents admitted that Molly had had a difficult time adjusting to her siblings. Now armed with that information, Molly's teacher worked with Molly and encouraged her to accept her siblings as special little people in her life. By the end of the school year, Molly had started to draw more colorful pictures.

While Molly openly turned the corner on her feelings about her siblings, the resentment of another young man, Jeremy, had long-term effects on a number of people. The first of four sons born to upper middle class parents, Jeremy received unlimited attention and all the perks and advantages a young child could ever want. He was the center of attention for almost four years before his brother Danny arrived. Early on, Jeremy resented Danny, and the sibling rivalry continued throughout their childhood into adult life. Danny excelled in school, received his master's degree with honors from a local university, and launched a career in hotel management, landing a plum first job out of state and moving up the ladder at a regular pace.

Jeremy had settled into a career unrelated to his brother's. Jeremy was earning the respect of his employers and coworkers, yet he felt unsatisfied. He decided to leave his established career and try to outdo Danny in his chosen field. Jeremy enrolled in Danny's alma mater and studied hotel and restaurant management. After receiving his degree with high honors, Jeremy accepted an offer to manage a hotel on the East Coast. One hotel led to another, each one bigger and more prestigious.

Despite doing well, earning an excellent salary, and being courted by executive search firms based on his first-rate resume, Jeremy was not satisfied that he had surpassed Danny's achievements.

The sibling rivalry continued for years, and finally it destroyed Jeremy's marriage when he left his wife to wage his career war in Hawaii, Danny's adopted turf. He desperately wanted to beat Danny at his own game. The rivalry ended abruptly, however, when soon after Jeremy's arrival, Danny abandoned his career to pursue his passion of sailing, in which Jeremy had no interest.

These examples underscore the importance of parents preparing any child in the family—but certainly the first-born child—for the arrival of a sibling. Siblings are more than our first family members in or near our own age group; they also represent the first friendships we develop at a young age.

First-born children, once others arrive in the family, are often saddled with the expectations of setting a good example, helping their mother with the younger children, and taking charge when mother and father are away from the home. Children who are blessed with a strong and healthy family are encouraged to become role models for each other, fostering traits such as respect, trust, morality, ambition, and the ability to work things out.

First-born children grow up fast. If parents push their first-born child to achieve too quickly, however, it can promote fear of disappointing the parents, and that fear of failure can hinder development through adult life. They often choose structured work environments and shield themselves by not being outgoing in their relationships.

With the first child, parents make unintentional mistakes because they are learning. In our family, for example, our first-born was a very needy child. How do parents curb that neediness? Certainly not by hitting the child; yelling and screaming are counterproductive too. The parents lose control, but if they say yes and mean it, or say no and mean it—even if it is not to the liking of the child—someday the child will see the value of that decision.

Our first-born, Lila, wanted to have everything, as many young children do. However, we would say to her, "What we have given you is all we can do, but we will always love you." Seeing what her friends had, this was always difficult to accept. But now, as an adult with children of her own, she looks back and appreciates our response. If you give your children everything, you kill their spirit and dry their desire to dream. You need to leave an unfulfilled sense of want and desire in the heart of a child, instilling the virtue of humility so that when they grow up, they can look forward to a healthy attitude toward possessions rather than having their hearts ruined by the constant desire for more.

St. John Chrysostom (the Goldenmouth) admonishes parents to raise their children in virtues, unfettered by wealth:

> "If from the beginning we teach them to love true wisdom, they will have greater wealth and glory than riches can provide. If a child learns a trade, or is highly educated for a lucrative profession all this is nothing compared to the art of detachment from riches; if you want to make your child rich, teach him this. He is truly rich who does not desire great possessions or surrounds himself with wealth, but who requires nothing.
>
> "Therefore wealth is a hindrance, because it leaves us unprepared for the hardships of life. So, let us raise our children in such a way that they can face any trouble, and not be surprised when difficulties come; let us bring them up in the discipline and instruction of the Lord."

Middle children

In families with an odd number of children, it is easy to determine who the middle child is, but in a large family, the distinction of the middle child becomes a bit fuzzy. One young woman told me she wishes she had not been born in the middle, because she always finds herself promoting peace between her older brother and younger sister or being the go-between when her siblings are at odds with each other. This is not unusual for middle children.

There are advantages and disadvantages to being born in the middle. Quite often, they are lost in the shuffle, receiving less attention than their older and younger siblings. In some cases, middle children resort to attention-getting devices, sometimes including bad behavior but more often by achieving something worthwhile. They tend to be outgoing, friendly, and agreeable. If the lack of attention has a negative effect on the middle child, he or she may suffer from a lack of self-confidence or from insecurity that could cloud judgment in adult life. Parents need to make a special effort to assure them that they do not always have to please everyone and to make them understand that their opinions matter. This will foster a greater feeling of acceptance and help them build self-confidence.

Last-born children

The children born last in the family, often called the babies, mirror the first-born in that they receive a lot of attention, but unlike their oldest sibling, they usually have fewer strict rules to guide their childhood. By the time the last-born arrives, the novelty of first-time achievements has subsided. When parents show little excitement over the last-born child's accomplishments, no matter how small, the child tends to take more risks, seeking novel approaches to doing things their siblings did more conventionally. If they grow up feeling that whatever they do does not matter, it can undermine their self-confidence. Every child deserves to be rewarded for their accomplishments, from their first spoken word to their first straight-A report card.

Some theorists claim that birth order has a profound effect on personality traits and relationships later in life; others maintain that the order of birth does not matter after the child leaves the family circle. Perhaps theorists will never agree totally on the importance of birth order.

Challenges

It is always difficult to raise children. There are two basic ingredients: parents must act as parents, and they must not try to be everything to all of their children. That is not what the child looks for. Later, when outside influences come to play, how do you deal with them? By having dialogue, talking about them, by telling your children, "Yes, you will see things that are ugly or that you are pressured to do."

Although the values of loyalty, responsibility, appreciation, respect, and love are important to teach children, even at a very young age, sacrifice is the most important. It is taught and caught by example. Sacrifice is embodied in paying attention, in listening, and in working hard to provide, to create a sense of peace.

My wife Nouhad may not say much, but when the children see what she has done for them, they know it was always through sacrifice. Children, who are raised in a home with everything but without a sense of sacrifice, grow up thinking of their parents as babysitters and buyers. There is no parent-child relationship.

Lila, our eldest, learned her mother's traits of respect, sacrifice, and charity. Our second child, Alex, is very ambitious. Both our first- and second-born have been blessed with their mother's serenity. They are very quiet but not introverted. They have embodied their mother's strengths, including self-confidence. The second two of our four children adopted my traits; they are very outspoken and very strong. So it is two for their mother and two for me.

Alexa, the "sandwich" child as I call her, could have been considered rebellious as a child. She always had a response to whatever we said to her. She knew many boundaries could not be crossed, but she tried hard to negotiate all of our rules, nonetheless.

Christa, the last child is a combination of her three siblings.

Not all first-borns become leaders; not all middle children are over-achievers; and not all last-born children are free-spirited. More important than their position of birth in the family is the blessing each child brings to the family. It is important for parents to cultivate that understanding in their children and to let each child know that they have a purpose in life to follow moral teachings, achieve goodness, and build valuable relationships. Being good morally leads to doing good practically.

Parents need to make sure that the feet of each child are firmly based on a path that will lead to a life of goodness. When they incorporate the sacramental life into the life of the family, the path may not be revealed completely, but the child will have a mystical, inner light that will show them what external path to follow.

Your children are not your children.
They are the sons and daughters of
life's longing for itself.
They come through you but not from you.
and though they are with you yet

they belong not to you.
You may give them your love but not your thoughts,
for they have their own thoughts.
You may house their bodies but not their souls,
for their souls dwell in the house of tomorrow,
which you cannot visit, not even in your dreams.
You may strive to be like them,
but seek not to make them like you,
for life goes not backward nor tarries with yesterday.

You are the bows from which your children
as living arrows are sent forth.
The archer sees the mark upon the path of the infinite.
and He bends you with His might
that His arrows may go swift and far.
Let your bending in the archer's hand be for gladness;
for even as He loves the arrow that flies,
So He loves also the bow that is stable.

Khalil Gibran
The Prophet

One final but very important note on this subject: As happy as parents are when their first child is born, it indeed complicates their relationship with each other, because a baby is distracting. Parents need to learn how to balance their relationship, keeping their romance and intimacy alive with handling the responsibilities of parenthood.

Memory Bank

Someone once told me that for every year we live, we pack a suitcase (sometimes a trunk) of memories— good and bad, happy and sad. Depending on our early life experiences, some of our memories might be peaceful or tormented. We bury the unpleasant memories beneath the happy ones, as if to forget they never happened, or at least should not have happened. Outsiders are often clueless about what makes for a child's unhappy memories, but their origins can be like Molly and Jeremy's dethroning experiences and the resentment that followed. Or they can be from witnessing or being victims of abuse, either emotional or physical.

Periodically, it is important for us to go as far back as memory permits, unpack those cases, sort out the memories, and discard those that no longer serve a purpose in our life. Treat the experience like depositing money in a bank, withdrawing funds you no longer need to save.

To a child, some memories carry more weight than others. For instance, moving to another city, state, or even to another country just as a child is venturing outside the family circle and interacting with other children can be traumatic to one who has not been adequately prepared for leaving a comfort zone. Some children consider a move to a new location an adventure; others are sad about leaving familiar sights and their first real friends.

The transition could become a pleasant experience with the parents' proper explanations: first, of the need for the move ("Daddy—or Mommy—got a great new job") and, second, of the importance for the family to support him (or her) and live near his (or her) new job,. There are no guarantees, however. With a little encouragement and even by making a game of the move, children can become flexible, appreciative of new challenges, and open to seeing new places and meeting new people. The memories attached to such a move, however, vary depending often on the age of the child, his or her fear of change, and how attached he or she has become to friends and places in their present home environment.

Who is the boss?

In today's world, it is not always easy to know who is making the decisions for a family. Some parents are more liberal, more inclined to let their children make decisions or determine their behavior long before they are equipped to understand the ramifications of their choices. In other situations, parents cede control of their children, and in so doing, they lose part of themselves.

Elizabeth and her husband Charles had three children, two girls and one boy. Elizabeth loved the finer things in life— beautiful china, crystal vases, and exquisite antiques. She displayed them tastefully throughout her house. During child-rearing years, she maintained the kind of household she loved, and by setting limits and establishing ground rules, her children never broke any of her fragile collectibles. In fact, they all grew up to appreciate them and enjoyed receiving these family treasures when their mother passed away.

Eleanor, in stark contrast, had four boys by her husband Harry, and they "raised hell" at home on long days when Harry was at work. Eleanor, like Elizabeth, loved beautiful artifacts and collected lovely china dinnerware and crystal vases and candelabra. Unfortunately, she did not tell her sons not to run and roughhouse indoors, because she did not want to inhibit their budding personalities. Instead, she allowed them to rule the roost. She put away her beautiful and fragile collectibles and replaced them with plastic counterparts. Her home resembled a campsite, save for comfortable couches and a few chairs.

Each mother approached parenting differently. Elizabeth believed, rightly so, that parents need to set limits to their children's behavior, realizing that discipline creates freedom; Eleanor thought setting limits would stifle her children's ability to express themselves. Which mother was right? Arguments have been made for both being right, but in a child's formative years, how can he or she know what is proper behavior, what boundaries must not be crossed, what values must be learned?

When a young couple first becomes parents, they are confused about when to tell their child something of importance, what kind of punishment is appropriate for misbehavior, and how much punishment is too much. Parents at this stage often make mistakes, some that negatively affect the child for many years.

Some parents drag their young children down a dark road that leaves them traumatized, often for life. James's parents practiced a particularly rigid, restrictive faith. James and his brother were denied all the joys of childhood—no toys, no birthday parties, no presents under a glittering Christmas tree. The father was abusive to the extreme that he even destroyed any animal that James befriended to prevent him

> A child needs to be listened to and talked to but not talked at. Teaching is not tyranny!

from becoming "soft." The mother was abusive in her own right, because she did not come to the defense or rescue of her children.

James's feelings of being unloved lingered throughout his teens, young adult life, and mature adult life. They hampered his ability to have meaningful relationships. He did not know how to love, because he felt unloved. He did not know how to show affection, because no one had ever hugged or kissed him. He still grapples with these problems. He disavowed his parents' religious beliefs, changed his faith a number of times, and completely dissociated himself from his birth family.

A child needs to be instructed but never destroyed (2 Corinthians 4:7-9). I tell parents, "If you want your children to respect you, respect them first."

Children learn not only by our words but by our deeds. As good as parents are, they make mistakes. Many are afraid to admit that they have made mistakes in raising their children. They are afraid to apologize. Some parents know how to apologize, to say, "I am sorry." Other parents have the courage to say, "I do not have the answer. I do not know, but we will figure it out together." That was my experience. If I did not know what to do, I would ask my children, "What would you like me to do?"

Children born of the same parents collect different memories from their childhood. One might have only happy recollections; another might harbor hard feelings about a domineering mother; and a third might recall the constant disapproval of a controlling father; yet all three children grew up in the same household with the same parents.

All of the events we have cited in this chapter prepare children for the next stage in building relationships: making friends in school, at church, and in the community. If the parents have heeded Proverbs 22:6, "Train up a child in the way he should go: and when he is old, he will not depart from it," they can anticipate a relatively smooth transition for their children as they embark on their exciting new frontier.

Points to Ponder

When was the last time you looked in the memory cases you packed in your childhood?

Are you harboring emotional wounds from your childhood?

Are you still resentful of how your parents treated you or of your siblings?

Have you forgiven your parent(s) for mistreatment, excessive punishment, even abuse?

Are you copying your parents' bad habits in raising your own children?

What positive influences did you receive from your parents?

If you are not an only child, what lasting impressions did you receive from your sibling(s)?

Do you consider yourself a good role model to your sibling(s)?

2

PUBERTY & PUPPY LOVE

"Love is sentimental measles."
Charles Kingsley

When we leave our family circle as youngsters and start to develop relationships, we realize how important they are in fulfilling our need for companionship. In a broader sense, we also need the community as a whole and, in part, the church family. In the Christian family, the seeds of spiritual enrichment are planted early. Parents equip their children with certain tools, the most important being prayer, but discovering the use of these tools makes for their own experiences.

Sometimes parents have to allow their children to make mistakes, for learning and relearning. No matter how much parents equip their children with the right values and qualities, they need room to embrace their own successes and failures. Children put into practice what they have learned and sometimes push the envelope. Then they get hurt and have to get back on the right path or they become lost.

Even when parents provide a strong foundation at home, children rebel. That rebelliousness brings choices, positive and negative. Many parents try to make their child conform, but doing so can break the spirit of the child. One woman told me that when she was a child, she often did the opposite of the rest of the family. Her mother used to ask her, "Why do you always have to be different?" Years later, after the daughter grew up and charted her own respected course in life, her mother said, "I am so happy you are not like everyone else!" The woman's mother had not broken her daughter's spirit when she was a girl and lived to honor her individuality. If children have a strong foundation, even in their rebellious years, it will become the net that will bring them to safety if they fall.

Puberty

It seems like yesterday when you saw your four-year-old nephew. How cute he was! Then the next thing you know, he is having a

> "Leave the nest to find your best, and God will do the rest."
> *Anthony Michaels*

party for his tenth birthday. Where did the time go, you ask yourself, and what happened to that cute little toddler?

It is all about puberty, one of the common denominators we all share. No one escapes puberty, although the changes that take place in puberty affect boys and girls differently, even within the same sex. The start of puberty varies, depending on genes, gender, and nutrition, but for girls, it usually begins around the age of seven and at nine for boys, and for both, it ends in the mid- to upper teens.

Puberty is about growth spurts, voice changes, curves, hormones, and puppy love. Puberty can also be a time of highly charged emotions, as hormones play new roles in young bodies and minds. It all starts with the brain's timely release of these hormones that launch so many changes, from growing taller to developing sexual and reproductive organs, from growing hair everywhere to having breasts and periods. These are all big changes that occur quickly. Moods change, emotions are fragile, and these pre-adolescents start to find their direction without constant parental supervision.

Puberty is the important interim stage in a person's life between childhood and adulthood, bridged slightly by adolescence, which tags onto the last years of puberty. During this stage when changes are happening quickly, some will develop slower or faster than others, but eventually puberty phases out. It is important for parents and friends to reassure these youngsters that their changes are normal and that their appearance makes them who they are, even if they do not have all of the outward manifestations of growth changes that some of their friends have. Individuality is to be applauded, both in looks and in personality, provided it is not extreme.

Puppy love

Along with hair and hormones comes that certain yet indescribable attraction toward a member of the opposite sex. It does not have to be confined to one our own age. Girls can have crushes on a handsome, mature schoolteacher, and boys can be attracted to a popular young singer or actress.

Larry and Sue were in the same third-grade class. Sue was shy, and Larry was uncharacteristically flirtatious. With Valentine's Day approaching, the teacher suggested that the students bring cards to exchange with their fellow classmates. When Valentine's Day arrived, some students received more cards than others received, but when Sue opened one card, she had the surprise of the day: tucked in the card was a ten-dollar bill! It was from Larry. Years later, Larry and Sue ran into each other, and Sue finally asked why he had given her the money. He replied, "I guess you could call it puppy love. I was quite taken by you."

Whomever the object is, the feeling is indeed referred to as puppy love or a crush, but it is really infatuation, another important contribution to our growth cycle. It is the first time we love someone outside our family, even though it is not to be confused with real love. Sigmund Freud recognized the power of early love, citing its validity as the "proverbial durability of first loves."

There is a downside to infatuation as we grow older. In extreme cases, infatuation can lead to stalking or even more dangerous behaviors. But in childhood, a crush on someone else serves as an innocent gateway to loving others.

During this sexual orientation phase, some boys and girls get carried away with their young loves, so it is important for parents to monitor what is happening and leave the door open for their children to talk to them about any of the changes they are experiencing.

Growing pains

In our school experiences, we encounter members of our peer group who conform to the values we hold dear and some who do not. We face conflicts, even on the playground, as bullies start to become more aggressive, and we learn to make decisions on our own about how to react to the good and bad behavior in others. If we rebel and follow the troublemakers, we make trouble for ourselves. Having a caring heart and a loving spirit, on the other hand, goes a long way toward cultivating the kind of relationships that can last a lifetime, and often do. Sometimes, however, those new, fragile friendships take a surprising turn, as in the following example.

Alfred, a fifth-grade student in a middle-class suburban community, was a loner. He rarely spoke to his classmates and never responded to the teacher when she called on him in class. He sat in solitude on the sidelines during recess and seemed to be content in his painful shyness.

One day, Alfred came to school with a completely different personality. He greeted his classmates, chuckled at their jokes, engaged in conversation, and participated in classroom discussions. What made him change overnight?

That same evening, he rode his bike along a divided highway to visit Margie, a classmate who had always given him the courtesy of a greeting or word of friendship, despite the silence that prevailed on his part. When he arrived at Margie's house, he asked to see her. She finished drying the dishes and then dashed out the front door to see Alfred still waiting by his bike. The two ten-year-olds talked for almost an hour. They parted that evening as friends, looking forward to seeing each other the next day at school.

When Margie arrived in class, however, the teacher informed the students that young Alfred had been killed in an accident the night before. Margie was stunned to hear the news, but she was even more puzzled why he had opened up the day before he died and why he had reached out to her in such a friendly way just before he was killed.

We never know when an act of friendship will touch another person's life. Alfred died knowing he had at least one friend, and most likely he died at peace, knowing that he had reached out in appreciation to his classmates, even for one day.

Some early friendships last a lifetime, and we have heard of budding romances that started as puppy love and led to a lifetime romance and marriage. Some friends never move far from where they grew up, and their early friendship remains intact and special throughout their lives.

Points to Ponder

Do you remember your very first friend?

Did your first friendship have a lasting effect on your life?

What was it about that friendship that stayed with you?

Do you know if you left a lasting impression on someone you knew in your childhood?

Did you ever like someone who didn't return the same feelings to you?

How did that lack of reciprocation affect you short-term and long-term?

When was the first time you witnessed discrimination or other improper treatment of a schoolmate or playmate?

How did you feel about that kind of treatment of a peer?

Have you kept in touch with anyone you met in your childhood?

How has your relationship grown or changed?

When did you first feel "puppy love" toward someone?

"The heavens were not made in God's image," he said,
"nor was the sun, nor the stars.
You alone are a copy of the Being
Who is above all things,
A similitude of the incorruptible Beauty,
And a reflection of the true Light.
In that image is our human glory and our greatest hope."

Meditation by St. Gregory of Nyssa

3

THE SECURITY
OF SHARED LOVE

"You are the only you God made.
God made you and broke the mold."
Max Lucado

One day a group of scientists got together and decided that man had come a long way and no longer needed God. They chose one scientist to tell God that they were done with Him.

The scientist walked up to God and said, "God, we have decided that we no longer need you. We are at the point where we can clone people and do many miraculous things, so why don't you go and get lost."

God listened very patiently and kindly to the scientist, and after he was done talking, God said, "Very well, how about this. Let us say we have a man-making contest."

"Okay, great!" replied the scientist enthusiastically.

But God added, "Now we are going to do this just like I did back in the old days with Adam."

"Sure," said the scientist. "No problem." He bent down and grabbed a handful of dirt.

God looked at him, shook his head, and said, "No, no, no! Get your own dirt."

This humorous story makes a good point to support the opening quote of this chapter. God made us out of His creative love for us. He gave us the gifts of life and of dignity. As Paul J. Wadell writes,

> "Living from the love and goodness of God frees us, because it means we do not have to make ourselves count. If my life is a gift, I do not have to establish its value and dignity. I do not have to make myself matter. If my life is a gift, I can live

free from fear and anxiety, because I matter most
to the 'gift giver.'"

Have you ever been given a gift wrapped beautifully and tied
with colorful satin ribbon? For a few moments, did you want just
to look at the gift, because it was too beautiful to open? Then,
when you looked inside, the gift was even more beautiful. God has
given each of us that kind of living gift, but we have to look inside
to see the real beauty of the gift, the gift of ourselves. We must
love the gift of us.

As Christians, when we understand who makes us, we accept
our life as a gift. By so doing, we no longer depend on any special
talent or ability to define us as persons. Even the worst and
poorest of us is a child of God.

We must rise from our circumstances, knowing that we are
not self-made. Our strength comes from God; our virtue comes
from a higher authority, our Lord.

It is God's nature to give life out of His love for all living
things. There is no end to His creative love. Just think: We live
because God loves us. Just like when friends tells us that our love
and support keeps them going, God's love does the same for us; it
keeps us going. As Wadell so aptly says,

"God does not create and then abandon us. God does not draw us to live only to leave us on our own. God's love is the gift from which everything is created and lives."

How can we not love ourselves when we know we were born from the love of God? Loving ourselves is not about being arrogant or conceited, asserts noted psychologist and social philosopher Erich Fromm. Instead, he proposes that "loving oneself means caring about oneself, taking responsibility for oneself, respecting oneself, and knowing oneself (being realistic about one's strengths and weaknesses). In order to truly love another person, one needs to first love oneself in this way."

The search for happiness

Self-knowledge, loving self, and understanding one's purpose in life are needed in order to succeed in finding happiness. The Christian perspective indeed is based on believing that we are creatures made in the image and likeness of God who sent Jesus to Earth to do His work.

Many books have been written about happiness, and there is even an institute of happiness. I am most happy when I feel that I have given my utmost.

In today's world, happiness is cloaked in many disguises: money, fast cars, spacious homes, and exotic vacations, yet they are fleeting doses of happiness. *As Christians, we desire the happiness that lingers, that fulfills our heart's desires, and that lasts.*

Happiness comes only when you are contented in your heart for being you and for touching someone else's life. You must be true to who you are right now. How did you touch that person's life? Were they inspired? Did they accomplish something worthwhile as a result of what you did for them? Did they listen to you? Otherwise, you will remain empty, and the only way you can fill this emptiness is with good. *Greed never leads to happiness.*

When you find people who are happy, they are well-rounded individuals. They are happy at home. They are happy at work. They are happy in their community. Happiness does not mean they do not face rainy days and down times. Happiness is inner joy that is born in them and is

> Happiness is the reward that comes our way when we have utilized our God-given gifts

reinforced by parents, pastors, and friends. They always look at the world as a good place.

"Love for others is the manifestation of love for self.
If you want to know what your love
for yourself looks like, look at your love for others.
When you love yourself this way,
you love God this way.
This relationship is the divine love triangle:
self, God, and others."

Marlon Hartley Lindsay

The divine love triangle Lindsay describes refers to the church doctrine of the Holy Trinity. As Bishop Ware of the Eastern Orthodox Church says,

> "Man is made in the image of the Trinity, and except in special cases he is not intended by God to live alone, but in a family."

Happiness comes with a great deal of accountability and responsibility too. As St. Paul wrote,

> "When I was a child, I spake as a child, I understood as a child, I thought as a child: but when I became a man, I put away childish things."
> *1 Corinthians 13:11*

And yet, sometimes a child will show us the way. I recently heard about a boy who, when he was just four years old, came upon a homeless man in the city park where the boy and his family were spending a summer day. The boy's mother said his heart was broken. He appealed to his mother to let him make sandwiches for street people.

For the next four years until today, he has made peanut butter sandwiches every day and, with his mother, has taken them to the park and fed the homeless. What a beautiful lesson! How many little boys would have rushed away to play, rather than do something good for others? He learned early in life that in order to feel good, we have to do good for others, not just for ourselves. In fact, the young people in our church make sandwiches twice a year and feed the poor and homeless people in Detroit.

> A child is no different than a bird that falls a few times before it learns to fly.

Unfortunately, instead of giving themselves to their church, to their schools, to their community, too many people today have become part of the movement of fear and defensiveness, even regression. They are afraid of the world, so they withdraw from the world. They refuse to send their children to school because schools are a bad influence. They reject television because it is a bad influence, and sports leagues for the same reason. When families regress, they deny their children the experiences that shape them. Alternative life experiences are needed to give a child balance.

Real friends, real happiness

With smart phones and the Internet, we are better connected but farther apart. We are texting instead of talking. Facebook replaces face-to-face conversations. None of these social networking opportunities replace the need for real, flesh-and-blood friends, with whom we can share good times and sadness, and whom we can hug, catch the twinkle in their eyes or the smile on their face.

If you have ever climbed a mountain with a seasoned mountain climber, when you reached the top, your companion rejoiced in your success as much as you did. In our quest for happiness, we need this kind of friend to be our companion, to guide and support us along our journey. As Paul Wadell says,

> "The Christian moral life is an ongoing training in happiness; it must be lived in communities and sustained in friendships. It requires people who care for one another, help one another, and look out for one another. That is what good friends and good communities do."

When you see an old friend you have not seen for months or even years, and you both take up where you left off without missing a beat, you realize how resilient friendship is; the bond of true friendship is unbreakable, because your happiness together was based on love and kindness toward one another.

This is what we meant when we said that to have friendship-based love, you must love yourself first. You must practice loving yourself before you can truly love another. No friendship can be complete if either person does not love himself first. Then when they become friends, they project in each other the same characteristics they find in themselves, and that is likely what attracted them to each other in the first place. Without loving yourself first, friendships are incomplete and unfulfilling in the happiness department.

Some people love God, but they fail to love themselves. They fail to acknowledge that they are God's temple, so they fail to take care of the outward appearance of the temple.

How to love yourself

Erich Fromm said that love is a decision, which means you have to *decide* to love yourself. You have to *decide* that you are worthy of love and success and happiness. You have to *decide* that you deserve a fulfilled life. If you do not make this decision and do not love yourself, you will not be able to reach the potential that God intends for you to achieve.

Do you remember falling in love for the first time? Your heart fluttered whenever the object of your love approached. A blush skimmed your cheeks, and your eyes sparkled. Now, turn those same falling-in-love feelings inward; fall in love with yourself, the good and the not-so-good, even if it means addressing your weaknesses so you can love yourself more. When you love someone, you do so without demanding change.

After you fall in love with yourself, you will want to grow your love. You do that by treating yourself the same way you treat your friends. You pay yourself compliments, you think positive thoughts about yourself and your efforts, and you treat yourself with the same kindness your friends love to receive from you. Learn to treat yourself, weaknesses and all, with compassion.

St. John the Goldenmouth stresses the link between unity in marriage and mutual (shared) love:

> "The other party thereafter is yourself,
> when you love,
> For this is friendship—that the lover and the
> beloved should no longer be two persons divided,
> but in a manner one single person,
> Something which can never happen except from
> love.
> Therefore, seek not your own,
> That you may find your own."

Loving yourself becomes even more natural when you nurture yourself spiritually and open yourself to be more compassionate and loving toward others. In Ephesians 5:25 and 28, we are told,

> "Husbands, love your wives, even as Christ also loved the church and gave himself for it. So ought men to love their wives as their own bodies. He that loveth his wife loveth himself."

A strong sense of knowing and loving yourself boosts your confidence, but you can expand it even further by seeking opportunities that will help you to become better at whatever you do and to trust your ability to make the right decisions.

Being appreciative of how you came to be and what you have become is vital to the growth process of loving

Gratitude is the heart of a good attitude.

yourself and then sharing love with others. One technique that might help you become more thankful involves counting your blessings. When you go to bed at night, make sure your room is quiet. Close your eyes and think about everything that happened to you that day or those blessings you received for which you did not have to pay anything (a free meal, an unexpected gift, a friendly greeting from a stranger, or unsolicited words of encouragement, and so on). Be thankful for each person who smiled at you or each time you felt good about committing a random act of kindness to a person or an animal. Counting these blessings is a peaceful way to fall asleep. An added benefit is waking up feeling rested and grateful the next morning.

Set aside some time to enjoy life, to relax and have fun. Make sure you know that you are worth this special indulgence. You might double-up on enjoying life while exercising, preparing nutritious meals, taking long walks in the park, walking in a gentle rain (be sure to step in the puddles), or having fun with friends.

Plant your own garden instead of waiting for
Someone to bring you flowers.
Veronica Shoffstall

Points to Ponder

When did you first know that your life was a gift from God?

How has that knowledge changed your life?

When was the last time you volunteered to feed the hungry or work in a homeless shelter?

How do you feel when you reach outside of yourself and do a good deed for someone else?

In your lifetime, you will spend more time with *you* than anyone else will. Would you want to spend that much time with *you*?

How would you have to change in order to want to spend that much time with yourself?

When was the last time you paid yourself a compliment for doing something worthwhile?

When did you last leave a job because it minimized you?

When was the last time you cast aside your worries and just had fun all by yourself?

When was the last relationship you left because it was toxic?

How often do you turn off the noise, shut off the cell phone, turn off the computer and sit, meditate, pray, and tap into the deep love inside of you? (Worship too can be a great aid.)

"Though you should name infinite treasures,
none of them is comparable to a genuine friend.

"A friend rejoices at seeing his friend,
And expands with joy. He is knit to him
With a union of soul that affords unspeakable pleasure.

"With a friend, one would bear
Even banishment; but without a friend
Would not choose to inhabit
Even his own country.

"With a friend, even poverty is tolerable,
But without him, both health and
Riches are intolerable."

St. John Chrysostom

4

THE FOUNDATION OF FRIENDSHIP

"My best friend is the one
who brings out the best in me."
Henry Ford

How important are friends? What value do friendships bring to

our lives? According to Aristotle, the Greek philosopher, even if you have worldly goods but no friends, you would not want to live. But some people do live without friends—self-appointed recluses, hermits, and loners who cannot seem to form any good and lasting friendships. We are not referring here to monks who live in monasteries; their lifestyle is not self-appointed but called by God.

David, in his mid-fifties, is one such loner. His parents are gone, and his only sibling passed away in childhood. David constantly whines that no one wants to be his friend. He desperately desires "meaningful relationships," even marriage. No matter how much advice he has received from clergy, psychologists, and acquaintances that he must be a friend in order to have a friend, he does not put the advice into practice, although he says he "understands" their advice. David is unsuccessful in his quest, because he is more interested in having people love him than in being the kind of person others will love without effort. "Wishing to be friends is quick work, but friendship is a low ripening fruit," said Aristotle.

All the benefits of friendship—trust, loyalty, justice, love, to name a few—come slowly, but they are worth the patience it takes to receive them over time. Some couples in my parish, for example, who have been married for many years, started out as friends. Now that their hair has turned white and their faces have become the wrinkled roadmaps of lives well traveled, they still hold hands, complete each other's sentences, and chuckle at one another's foibles. They learned the value of waiting for the fruit of friendship to ripen.

Three kinds of friendship

The Greek word *philia* (literally "brotherly love") describes the inclusivity of friendship; a variety of friendships such as those between co-workers, families, neighbors, children, the church, and the larger community. Aristotle further divides friendship into three categories within philia: utility, pleasure, and virtue.

A friendship of utility is based on one person using the friendship for his immediate gain, not for lasting friendship. Perhaps he needs a boost in his career or some advantage in life that the other person can give him; no matter what the reason, this kind of friendship is based on selfishness.

A young woman involved in a serious relationship once told me that every time she performed a good deed for a friend, her significant other asked, "What's in it for you?" He didn't understand how she could give of her time and talents without charging a fee. She did not want to have a friendship of utility; she just wanted to help someone who needed help.

Friendships of utility are doomed. As soon as the person using the other gets what he wants, he moves on. He is not a just person because he receives an undeserved benefit from this brief relationship. In short, he is a user.

Aristotle's second kind of friendship is one of pleasure, but this type is generally mutual. When two people share a common activity, like fishing or cooking, they enjoy each other's company for the primary purpose of engaging in their favorite activity. They do not develop deeper ties, such as learning how they feel about important issues or what family problems they have. Like friendships of utility, the friends of pleasure simply give and receive pleasure. Aristotle also considered this friendship unjust because it is based only on what each one wants and nothing more. For that reason, this kind of friendship does not last long, either.

The third kind of friendship is one of virtue, which is the only kind that has staying power. The people involved in this kind of friendship love each other but not for what they can gain from each other. They help each other, care about what each other needs, and support each other in trying times. Because each one gives and receives and enjoys having the other person as a friend, those components (utility and pleasure) make their friendship whole, but only because they are attracted to each other's real character. They want to do things for each other out of love, and so their friendship is genuine and long-lasting. "My best friend is one who in wishing me well wishes it for my sake," said Aristotle.

Justice is necessary for a friendship to be complete. Justice enables a person to be concerned about his friend's happiness. Being just means always doing the right thing and doing things for others without expectation of anything in return. Justice is the glue that keeps a friendship of virtue together. That kind of friendship lasts a lifetime.

In fact, some of the most important friendships are those we make when we are young. Many people retain their early school-age friendships, even if

> "A true friend reaches for your hand and touches your heart."
> *Heather Pryor*

distance separates them. Still others, who made friends early on, continue to live in the same town, marry mutual school friends, raise their children, and live the remainder of their lives in close contact. Even their children grow up to become friends. How many times have you heard someone say, "You can choose your friends but not your relatives?" That is one of life's truisms. There are some things we cannot choose, like the families we are born into or their socioeconomic class, but we can choose who we want to have as friends.

Friendships are possible, according to Wadell, only when we willingly open our lives to others. He writes:

> "Friendships begin when we make room for other people in our lives. All our friends were once strangers, and the only way they changed from being a stranger is that we made space for them in our lives just as they did for us in their lives. To enter a friendship is to send out a signal that we are willing to adjust our lives for the sake of another. The only way we can grow is by risking the hospitality that makes space for others in our lives."

It does not matter how friendships are made, by choice or by chance. We need them because a life of goodness and happiness depends on having certain relationships. We cannot just be onlookers; we must include God and others; a life of community gives birth to other relationships. We need people to share our vision, agree with us on the important issues of life, and join us in our pursuit of a good and virtuous life. We want the guidance and support of friends not just in our quest for goodness, but because we need them. In significant ways, our moral life is built, in part, on the mutual desire of friends to be good.

In some areas of society, parents place strong emphasis on the importance of higher education, professions such as medicine, law, and engineering, and careers that can produce great monetary benefits. Even though their children acquire them, they may remain lonely; they invest in themselves and forget to include others.

Friends are the quintessential requirement for our lives because we cannot obtain virtues without them. The moral life is a cooperative partnership; it happens when we grow, change, and develop over the years through the most formative relationships in our lives. We need to grow on a daily basis and reinforce growth in those we love. As we read in 2 Peter 1:5, "And beside this, giving all diligence, add to your faith virtue, and to virtue knowledge."

Friendship and our moral development

Friends contribute to each other's moral development in three significant ways: 1) they form important character virtues and qualities in us, 2) they open us up and teach us to care for others, and 3) they deepen our capacity for life's most essential virtues.

Let us look at each way in greater depth. In the first way, good and lasting friendships, perhaps through mutual support, foster qualities of character such as caring, generosity, patience, thoughtfulness, kindness, self-control, sympathy, and forgiveness.

We grow morally; we develop our character, and we acquire virtues that are vital for a more fulfilling life.

Secondly, in seeking the good of the friend, which is the basic activity of a just friendship, we turn our attention from ourselves in order to serve the needs and interests of another. Each friend wants the best for the other, and they work to make it possible. We cannot be indifferent or halfhearted in our commitment to another's good. The main focus must be on the good and happiness of that friend.

The third way that friends help each other to become good is by teaching the value of faithfulness, of being truthful and trustworthy. Once we accept the responsibilities that go with friendship, we project ourselves into our friend's life out of empathy for what is happening to him and to put ourselves in his shoes. (I maintain that the world would be a far better place if more people practiced this one step—putting themselves in the other person's shoes, looking at his problem from his perspective. This is the "Golden Rule.")

We need friends to share life's ups and downs, in celebration and sorrow, in happiness and heartache, and in poverty and plenty. Friends establish a mutual dependency based on loyalty, trust, and presence, but doing so is not automatic or easy.

After a bone-weary day at work, have you ever found yourself pacing the halls of a hospital, supporting your best friend whose child was undergoing emergency surgery? Times like these are not easy, but they go with the territory of a true friendship. It is much easier and more enjoyable to be there for our friends when they are happy and upbeat. However, the test of friendship is when we help them to face life's challenges and heartbreaking circumstances. Patience and faithfulness are important virtues not only in these situations but also in dealing with the imperfections that all of us have.

Knowing us better than we know ourselves

Earl and Stephen became close friends when they attended the same university. They shared the same interests, as well as similar values and principles. The more time they spent together, the more they became like each other. Earl had a gift of public speaking but did not develop that gift; in fact, he would not acknowledge that he had such a gift. Stephen was always encouraging him to speak at city council meetings when they were passionate about a certain local issue, or to lead their adult Sunday school class.

One day, Earl received an unexpected opportunity at work to speak before a large group of corporate executives. He organized his notes carefully, made his speech thoughtfully, and received thunderous applause afterward. Later he related the incident to Stephen and confessed, "I think you knew me better than I knew myself." Stephen had encouraged Earl to own his gift, and in so doing, Earl went on to become a fine motivational speaker. Stephen was an important source of self-knowledge to Earl and thereby contributed to his moral development. Others can see in us what is hidden from ourselves.

> A friend is someone who believes in you even when you have ceased to believe in yourself.

Paul Wadell writes,

> "Friends aid our understanding of ourselves because by observing their character, we glean some sense of our own. If I see how love, goodness, and kindness are embodied and expressed in my friend, I can come to a better sense of how those same virtues are embodied and expressed in myself because of what I share in common with my friend."

Our self-knowledge is limited; sometimes our inability (or lack of desire) to admit our less likeable attitudes and habits thwarts our forward journey toward the good. Our friends can help us by being truthful, by telling us what we need to hear, and not just what we want to hear. This is how a true friendship works; it is a two-way street. One day, one friend might have to address the negative attitude of his friend, and the next time, he might have to call his friend up short on his stubbornness. All this takes place in a friendship built on mutual trust, or it would not work. Strengths and shortcomings are in each of us, and our best friends, including those we have married, must have the freedom to express themselves frankly about one another. That is how we grow toward the good. By being honest, we encourage that growth in each other.

Friendship means taking risks. We can confront a friend with his or her problem, but we risk losing the friendship in the process.

"A friend is one that knows you as you are,
understands where you have been,
accepts what you have become, and,
still, gently allows you to grow."
William Shakespeare

Good friends help us stay committed to our chosen course, to what is best for us and for our quest of goodness and happiness. As Wadell says,

> "In the Christian moral life, the quest can be disheartening. The goodness we seek is hard to attain and never fully in our grasp. We grow in this goodness, but we never completely possess it, because the goodness is the unexcelled goodness of God. Our quest always seems unfinished. Whether through humor, counsel, or simply their faithful presence, Christians should do for one another what good friends always do: They should help one another remain resolute in the pursuit of the most promising good for our lives."

We need friends to give us what we are unable to give ourselves. We are not alone; we are part of a community, and we cannot reach goodness and happiness without friends and community.

A bridge to greater love

In a small Midwestern city, two families gathered around the bassinette holding a tiny infant named Ellen. In the group was Joey, a curious two-year-old. He had never seen a baby before, and its tiny features fascinated him. The families enjoyed their time together, and when Joey and his parents prepared to leave, the little boy spoke up, "Can I have the baby?"

As it turned out, by fate or God's plan, Joey and Ellen saw each other on many occasions during their formative years. They attended the same schools, and although two years apart in age, they eventually graduated from the same high school. They were close friends all through their childhood and adolescence.

Ellen lived with her widowed mother, and they eventually relocated to a nearby large city. Joseph (which he preferred as an adult) went off to college in New England. They had not seen each other in quite some time. Joseph graduated and found a good job in the same city where Ellen lived. A mutual friend of theirs informed Joseph that, in fact, she lived nearby.

He called on her and immediately proposed, and Ellen accepted. Their bond of friendship had remained intact through separation, relocation, and other life changes. They married, had four children, and shared a wonderful Christian moral life. Building a marriage on a firm foundation of friendship, as Joseph and Ellen did, affirms the value of pre-marital friendship.

John Gottman, the renowned marriage expert, cites evidence to support this point. When asked what determines their satisfaction with sex, romance, and passion, 70 percent of wives and 70 percent of husbands said it was the quality of their friendship.

Points to Ponder

On what basis do you consider someone a friend?

How did your friendship start?

What qualities attracted you to him or her?

How do you show your friend that you value his/her friendship?

Have you ever initiated a friendship of utility? How long did it last? How did you feel about it later?

Has anyone ever initiated a friendship of utility with you? How did it make you feel?

Do you have friendships of pleasure?

What makes them different from utility friendships?

What makes them the same?

Why is a friendship of utility or pleasure not enough?

Why do they not last?

How many friends of virtue do you have? What brought you together?

What keeps your relationship strong with them?

How have you felt when a good friend pointed out a shortcoming of yours? How has he felt when you did the same thing to him?

"Don't rush into any kind of relationship.
Work on yourself first,
experiencing yourself and loving yourself.
Do this first, and you will soon attract
that special loving other."

Russ von Hoelscher

5

TAKING LOVE SERIOUSLY

*"He who is filled with love
is filled with God himself."*
Saint Augustine

Puppy love and friendship love are important growing steps that lead to serious love and marriage. Some couples, like Joseph and Ellen in the previous chapter, knew each other all their lives before they married. It did not require much thought, therefore, when the time was right for him to propose marriage. They knew in their hearts that they loved each other, valued their years of friendship, and shared their quest for goodness.

In today's high-tech world, taking love seriously takes on new meaning. I recently saw a quote by a young man who said that it took only a short while for him to know that he had found the right woman. They were seriously in love and looking forward to getting married one day. How did he know that? "We've been texting and sharing everything on Facebook for weeks now," he said. "We just know we are meant for each other. We hope to meet soon."

Joseph and Ellen fell in love the old-fashioned way over many years. Is it possible for today's young people to know so quickly that the one they meet through social networking is the right one for them, without ever seeing that person is real life? It sounds like "love at first sight." For some, it works, but for the majority, the longer the friendship or courtship, the better equipped both individuals will be to face the challenges of married life together.

In a 2011 New York Times article that discussed the ages at which men and women marry today, it was revealed that the average age for women is twenty-seven and for men, twenty-nine. They are getting their education and establishing their career before taking the important marriage step. Unlike past generations, the average American makes several important decisions by the time he or she marries. Marriage no longer represents the beginning of adult life, as it did with their parents and grandparents. Instead, marriage has become a merging of two adults.

I encourage young people to live and enjoy life for a few years and not rush into marriage. The New York Times article, in fact, supports this advice, at least for women. It notes that every year a woman delays marriage up to her early thirties, her chance of divorce decreases.

Communication in intimate relationships

Men and women utilize different techniques when they communicate with each other. For both sexes, there are some communication stumbling blocks that prevent them from having a better intimate relationship. In order to improve their communication with women, men need to give non-verbal feedback by smiling, nodding their head to show they are listening, and using more eye contact to demonstrate their attentiveness. Men should talk less about their own interests, interrupt less, and become better listeners. Women want them to be gentler in their caresses, and to cuddle and hug more. Finally, men need to show more emotion and become more comfortable with the give-and-take of praise.

Women need to acknowledge that men are not mind readers. Women need to offer what they want in a loving, direct way. Neither spouse should bring up unpleasant experiences from the past. If a man does not open up, his wife should assure him that she is there for him whenever he is ready to talk about sensitive issues. Nagging does not help. If the wife has a problem and asks her husband for help, she needs to know that he does not

> Women want most to be heard. Men want to fix things.

want to hear endless talk about her feelings on the matter; just let him tackle the problem directly. Men's conversations tend to concentrate less on feelings and more on tangible things like cars and activities such as sports and jobs.

By learning to understand these valuable insights into improving communication with your partner, both of you can realize increased happiness in your intimate relationship.

What is love?

If you do not know the ingredients of love, you limit love only to sexual attraction. Most people think of love in the romantic context, but romantic love cannot exist alone; it needs other ingredients. So when people are patient, when they sacrifice, when they communicate well, when they understand when to comfort and when to move away, when they understand mutual respect and mutual admiration, they understand that the totality of these ingredients is love.

Trying to define love takes away its mystery. Love is real; love is complex. Love means many things to many people. In 1 John 4:8, we learn that "God is love," and in Jesus's teachings, He encourages his followers to love one another and put love into real deeds, such as healing the sick, feeding the hungry, forgiving the sinner, visiting prisoners, and being inclusive to any and all.

The love that gave us life gives us others to enjoy our lives more fully. Wadell says that Christians understand love by considering why humans have been given the vocation to love.

> "More than anything, we have confirmed that love is what we are brought into existence to do and ought to be what we learn to do best, because love is what makes us like God. God is love, and we enjoy the happiness that is God if we become love too. If the Christian moral life is training in

happiness, it cannot overlook the central importance of love. Love is the language of God."

According to the fruits of the Holy Spirit, love goes through different stages and depths of feeling: attraction, infatuation, communion, intimacy, submission, passion, and ecstasy.

We hear that "opposites attract," but what is attraction? It comes from being ourselves, being natural, being the real deal. That applies to personality as well as physical appearance. I believe some men do not want women to wear makeup. They prefer the natural look. Inner and outer beauty has authenticity that cannot be copied.

Infatuation occurs when two people are intensely attracted to each other or one to another and that attraction makes them feel extraordinary.

When two people are in love, they enter into a communion during which they give to and take from each other those qualities that complement their own. Their very souls connect. This is known as projection.

In true intimacy, body merges with body, and spirit with spirit. Sexual energy and spiritual energy are recognized as the same.

Submitting to another person is the best way to find your true self. At last, you relinquish any notion of separation. Surrender is the result of letting go of the ego's last claims to separation. As you let go, something wonderful happens, and you are never the same again.

Passion is an interesting word. There is passion for life, passion for certain activities; there is even a passion fruit! Passion for life and love are the same; just as the heart of life is love.

Ecstasy is the state from which we come—the state of grace to which we shall eventually return. Ecstasy, the final stage of intimacy, comes when the spirit flows through love.

A safety net

We know that attraction to one another is the first criterion of falling in love, but as projection gives way to reality, infatuation is replaced by compassion and acceptance. Fierce passion turns into commitment for each other, by caring for each other, and by nurturing each other. If you allow for love at first sight, romance for couples is generated in a very instant way, but does it have legs to stand on? How do they communicate? Do they have a safety net to catch them if they fall?

In the West, there is a debate about how long a couple should date before they seriously consider marriage. I encourage couples to date for a period of fifteen months to two years. A longer period of dating will deviate from the purpose of marriage, because no matter how long we date, we always present ourselves in a reserved manner. All of our shortcomings may not surface, but, in time, they will. What will be revealed immediately will be what you value. What is your dream? What is your understanding of family? What is your understanding of forgiveness?

> We have replaced faces with Facebook.

In the non-industrialized world, men and women do not date. They believe that love will be born out of sacrifice and commitment in the future. Almost 90 percent of arranged marriages endure, but that does not mean the couples are happy.

We need to refocus on the issue of dating. It is an exhaustive experience for the young couple, trying to find the right person in an environment that puts pressure on young people to date and get married. (Approximately 65 percent of couples today meet through an online dating service, while 14 percent say they met through social networking—they have replaced faces with Facebook—but there is nothing like real-life interaction between two people.)

In the church community, we provide events for young people to become involved and get to know each other. My daughter

Alexa went to camp when she was thirteen or fourteen. Marc was fifteen. A priest drove them to camp. Lila, our first-born, had a similar experience with the late Jason. At the end of camp, Jason returned home and told his mother, "I have found my future wife." He said that without telling Lila or without having had a relationship with her.

These things happen. We should not lose sight of the mystery of the human relations. Sometimes we try so hard to figure out everything, we become exhausted. And when we find the answer, we are disappointed. Nothing is left to the imagination.

Love at the center of everything

Being a Christian means doing everything with love—thinking, talking, playing, and working.

> "Love suffers long and is kind; love does not envy; love does not parade itself, is not puffed up; does not behave rudely, does not seek its own, is not provoked, thinks no evil; does not rejoice in iniquity, but rejoices in the truth; bears all things, believes all things, hopes all things, endures all things. Love never fails." *1 Corinthians 13:4-8 NKJV*

Wadell points to three characteristics of God's love: 1) "to love something and find it good" 2) "to wish good for all living things," and 3) "to be steadfast, patient, and faithful."

When God created the world, He saw that it was good. When we love another person, we celebrate their existence. Goodness opens us up and draws us out of ourselves. We become agents of God's love, and He gives us the freedom to be creative and responsible agents of His love.

Love is to want everything to flourish and everyone to prosper, to wish the greatest goodness and excellence that is possible for them. In a sense, love is universal benevolence, but it is more than wishing all things well. "Love is a heartfelt commitment to seek, work for, and faithfully promote what is best for another," writes Wadell.

God's love endures. It never ends, even if we stop loving Him. He is ever faithful to us, even in our unfaithfulness. As Wadell says,

> "The only way that human love, like God's, can last is if we are willing to be patient, steadfast, faithful, and forgiving with one another."

If friendships stand the test of time, it is because both parties made the commitment to work through the hard times and setbacks. This is the cost of love. Most people love but do not know the cost involved in loving others. The cost of this close bond is paid in our own self-sacrifice, out of our own blood, and in so doing we mirror Christ's sacrifice for His Bride.

St. John Chrysostom writes in his commentary on Ephesians 5:21-33 of Christ's steadfast, self-sacrificing love for his Bride, the Church. St. John holds this as the high model, which our marriages are meant to reflect.

> "Whatever kind of woman you have chosen, you cannot have chosen anyone like the spouse Christ has chosen in marrying the church. And if she is different from you, it is not so different as the church is from Christ. Even so, he has not hated her, or loathed her for her terrible deformity. You want to know the extent of her deformity? Then listen to Paul, 'You were one time darkness' (Ephesians 5:8). Do you see how obscure she was? What is more obscure than darkness?
>
> "See too how brazen-faced she was. 'We were passing our days in malice and iniquity' (Titus 3:3). And how unclean: 'We were foolish and disobedient.' What I mean to say is she was a fool and a blasphemer, and yet, despite that, he sacrificed himself for that deformed spouse as if she had been beautiful, most deserving of love, marvelous. Full of admiration, Paul exclaims, 'One will hardly die for a righteous man, yet Christ died for us while we were still sinners.' (Romans 5:7-8).

"After taking a spouse like that, he made her beautiful and he washed her. He did not shrink even from that. He did it 'that he might present her to himself in splendor.' With water he washed her uncleanliness away, water accompanied by the word. What word was it? 'In the name of the Father, the Son, and the Holy Spirit.' He not only adorned her, he made her resplendent 'without spot or wrinkle or any such thing.'"

We too, in our spouse, seek this beauty. It could be that we are in a position to create this beauty ourselves. Do not ask of your wife what is not in her power. Note carefully that the church received everything from the Lord. It was He who made her resplendent without spot or wrinkle.

We make promises to love, knowing that at some point, love asks more than we can give. Only through cultivating the virtues of patience, fidelity, forgiveness, and reconciliation, and emboldened by Christ's example, can we move through the darker times and emerge in the light of love's promise.

Moving forward

When two people experience serious love, they consider marriage the next step. Some couples delay this step for a long time, even years. If the couple is grounded in a Christian moral life and active in their church family, they should be better equipped to make a decision about marriage whenever they feel the time is right.

Couples who do not have the Christian orientation or faith to direct them might use other means to help them decide if their relationship should go to the next level. Even after that decision is made, they can still check their decision against a chart to tabulate the pros and cons of their relationship. List all the things that are positive about the decision to marry in the PRO column, and all the negative attributes in the CON column. If the CON column outweighs the PRO column, it might be time to reconsider. This is not a foolproof way of making a major decision like marriage, but it could present red flags that might not be apparent otherwise.

Other points to consider before reaching the marriage proposal stage include making sure neither of you has emotional baggage from childhood (or later years) that might affect your relationship negatively. For most couples, however, this is revealed in marriage. Much of our emotional baggage is hidden in our unconscious. It is unrealistic to believe anyone has no emotional baggage. Perhaps acknowledging and dealing honestly and openly with the baggage is what is needed. There is always more to come.

Another point is for the partners to be honest with each other, which will help to build trust in their relationship. Other things to consider before taking the big plunge are sharing responsibilities, even before the marriage subject arises; lifting each other up instead of criticizing or belittling them; and facing the fact that not every relationship is meant to be or to lead to marriage. If the latter becomes obvious, then exit gracefully.

> Love might seem to be magic, but sometimes magic can be an illusion.

Points to Ponder

When did you first know that your feelings for partner were serious? How did you know?

Did your partner feel the same way about you? If not, when did he or she feel the same way as you did?

What especially attracted you to each other?

How long did you date before you realized your feelings were serious for each other?

Has anything about your partner's personality, attitudes, behavior given you pause?

Have you and your partner discussed your strengths as well as your shortcomings?

Do you and your partner share the same religion, values, and principles?

Have you and your partner discussed any differences in beliefs, values, and principles and how they might affect your marriage?

Have you and your partner discussed sex and when to start a family?

Would you want to marry someone who didn't share your desire to have a family?

"Today we will concern ourselves primarily with sacramental marriage. We will consider how marriage can contribute to our spiritual life. We know that marriage is an institution established by God. It is "honorable" (Hebrews 13:4). It is a "great mystery." (Ephesians 5:32) An unmarried person passes through life and leaves it; but a married person lives and experiences life to the full."

Father Aimilianos of Simonopetra

6

MARRIAGE:
THE SACRED UNION

"Marriage is not a noun; it's a verb.
It isn't something you get.
It's something you do.
It's the way you love your partner every day."
Barbara DeAngelis

"Will you marry me?" are perhaps the four most eagerly

anticipated words a young woman wants to hear. Four words do not a marriage make, however, but acceptance changes life forever. To be fully prepared for marriage, partners need to evaluate themselves individually and collectively. Will their strengths help them weather the storms of married life; will their weaknesses cause problems long after the wedding cake has been cut?

The most critical preparation for marriage involves developing each other's virtues. Let us consider what we mean by the word virtue. It is derived from Latin, meaning moral strength, excellence, and worth. The dictionary defines it as moral excellence, goodness, and righteousness. It notes the cardinal virtues such as prudence, justice, fortitude, and temperance; as well as the theological virtues of faith, hope, and charity. So when marriage partners help each other's virtues, it means they encourage the goodness and moral excellence and promote the strengths and talents of each other.

Remember how Stephen helped his friend Earl recognize his talent for speaking? Earl had not acknowledged that talent, but with his friend's prompting, he went on to become a motivational speaker. Just as friends help each other develop talents, so must couples help each other grow their virtues—honesty, justice, love, patience, compassion, generosity, prayer, worship, and forgiveness. Why are virtues so important? Wadell says we cannot have a good and flourishing life without them.

"...through them we move from simply being oriented...to the good...to consistently embodying and doing the good and even flourishing in the good. Through the virtues, we become good persons who know what it means to live a good life."

No couple wants to think about the difficulties that might lie ahead after they get married, but it is unwise to ignore these potential pitfalls. The Apostle Paul even speaks to this:

"Are you bound to a wife? Do not seek to be free. Are you free from a wife? Do not seek marriage. But if you marry, you do not sin, and if a girl marries she does not sin. Yet those who marry will have worldly troubles, and I would spare you that."
1 Corinthians 7:27-28

In order to be fully equipped to handle whatever befalls them, however, the married couple needs virtues like courage, hope, patience, and perseverance. These particular virtues will enable the couple or one of the spouses to face a major calamity such as terminal illness, financial ruin, or even the untimely death of a spouse.

Father Aimilianos addresses the hardships of married life:

"Marriage, then, is a journey through sorrows and joys. When the sorrows seem overwhelming, then you should remember that God is with you. He will take up your cross. It was he who placed the crown of marriage on your head. But when we ask God about something, he doesn't always supply the solution right away. He leads us forward very slowly. Sometimes he takes years. We have to experience pain, otherwise life would have no meaning. But be of good cheer, for Christ is suffering with you, and the Holy Spirit, 'through your groanings is pleading on your behalf.'" *Romans 8:26*

> No overnight FedEx delivery brings virtues to your door.

Becoming a virtuous person takes time and practice, even though we have the innate capacity for virtue. What makes our virtues grow is putting them into use, and then they become habits. If we want to increase our virtue of patience, for instance, we must become patient with our spouse. If we want to develop our virtue of hope, we must not give up when the slightest setback occurs. If we want to be courageous, we must show courage to others who are struggling.

Virtues can grow only in a humble heart. Humility is the foundation of all virtues, according to St. Anthony the Great.

Certainly married couples want to develop these virtues because they want to live a good life with each other. There are also vices—greed, envy, jealousy, and revenge—that married or about-to-be-married couples need to recognize and work to eliminate from their lives. These vices are toxic habits that can prevent them from achieving the very happiness they seek. Putting a priority on monetary gain, being materialistic, harboring jealousy, or settling an old score ahead of one's marriage turns the person away from the good and makes him a poor candidate for a spouse.

More than a wedding

Getting married is not just about planning a wedding, although it may well be the first major collaboration the couple makes. Getting married involves making sure you know each other and yourself, defining your life goals, and learning to know more about each other on a deeper level.

Are you flexible? Do you really listen to what your intended spouse wants? Can you compromise when the two of you reach a roadblock? Are you able to maintain a sense of humor during this somewhat stressful premarital stage? Communication plays a vital role in this stage; it is important to pay keen attention to how you and your betrothed exchange ideas, discuss problems, and handle outside interference from family members and close friends.

The more a couple concentrates on strengthening their assets and works to turn their weaknesses into strengths, the better their chances will be as they start married life together. The happiest couples follow the "preference role"; that is, the role that each does best. Knowing where each one stands on important issues that they will face as a married couple—such as who will handle the budget and finances, when to start having children, how often to pray together or where to attend church, and how to set boundaries with in-laws and other "new" family members—will get them off on the right foot. It cannot be overstated that honest, direct communication about these issues and many others at this juncture is imperative to success in marriage. No one wants to be blindsided about important issues after they get married.

After you have proposed, and your intended has said "yes," life will never be the same again. Both of you will embark on a journey that will be uniquely yours, because as a couple you merge your individual traits and values that will make your marriage truly special. You will use these traits and values to face difficulties, cope with differences, manage anger, enhance spiritual beliefs, and forge a commitment to help make your marriage survive and thrive.

You may also find that you and your spouse make a perfect match; no matter what challenges you face, you seem to know how to handle them. But sometimes a perfect match is not so desirable. Sometimes a *harmonious combination* of traits in varying degrees of difference bodes well for success in marriage.

> "My soul takes pleasure in three things,
> and they are beautiful in the sight of the
> Lord and of men:
> Agreement between brothers,
> friendship between neighbors,
> and a wife and husband who live in harmony."
> *Sirach 42:9-10*

To Christians, marriage means a lifetime of faithful commitment between two people. St. Paul compares marriage to the relationship between Christ and His Church. Just as God loves each of us equally and without limit, this very same kind of love is what is necessary in marriage. Just as He is committed to each one of us, He expects the same faithful commitment between man and woman when they marry. The monogamous nature of Christian marriage excludes polygamy, adultery, and lustful fantasies of others. If the couple is serious about their Christian commitment in marriage, they will be oblivious to the sex-oriented temptations in the world and maintain their sacred covenant with one another.

With monogamy comes the freedom to know one's beloved through mutual care and growth, going beyond the flesh and into the spirit. Because we continually change and grow in our relationship with one another, acquiring knowledge of each other takes a *lifetime*, even eternity.

Christian marriage, a conjugal union, is blessed by God through the sacramental ritual of the wedding ceremony. Grace is bestowed on them to create within their union a divine calling to become one flesh and procreate in perfect love and devotion.

> "Nevertheless, neither is man independent of woman, nor woman independent of man, in the Lord. For as woman came from man, even so man also comes through woman; but all things are from God." *1 Corinthians 11:11-12 NKJV*

Cohabitation

The U. S. government defines cohabitation as two unrelated adults of the opposite sex sharing the same dwelling. The all-too-common practice of today's young people cohabiting (living together) prior to or instead of marrying is fueled by the prevalence of movie stars and other public figures opting to live together and even have children before marriage or otherwise outside of marriage.

Cohabitation seems to allow for increased intimate time together as a couple without the commitment of marriage. Some couples believe it is necessary to test their compatibility and learn more about each other without worrying whether their marriage will end in divorce if they do not get along. There may be some economic advantages; in fact,

> Half of all couples today cohabit before marriage.

recent income tax hikes for married people are driving some couples to opt for cohabitation.

Across demographic lines (race, age, socioeconomic class), more and more people are choosing cohabitation. Some of them have been married and divorced, and they prefer not to enter into a marital commitment again. If both cohabiting partners have a college education, the chances improve that they will marry and remain married for at least ten years. Cohabitation is more prevalent among those with less than a high school education.

Due to strict laws, cohabitation was almost impossible prior to the 1960s. How times have changed! According to the U. S. Bureau of Census (2003-4), half of all couples cohabit before marriage, and 40 percent of children before the age of sixteen will live in a cohabiting family. Over 50 percent of couples who first cohabited ever get married; couples who live together are not only at greater risk of divorce but also divorce earlier in their marriage.

Another concern about cohabitation is the birthrate, which spiked to 53 percent in the late 1990s, up from only 29 percent a decade earlier. In those relationships, when the child is just two years old, 30 percent of the couples are no longer living together. The United States has the distinction of all Western countries of having the lowest rate of children being raised by both biological parents—63 percent.

Despite all of the strikes against cohabitation, it is fast becoming the arrangement of choice for today's young couples for a number of reasons, among them: insecurity, a trial run for marriage, emancipation from family, convenience, housing need, financial concerns, "free" sex, and a belief that marriage is not a healthy institution.

In Christianity, Judaism, and Islam, cohabitation is considered a violation of moral tenets. While some individuals in those faiths likely contribute to the high rate of cohabitation, it is a serious matter. Living outside of the Christian sacrament of marriage should be reason enough not to engage in cohabitation, but there are other reasons too. Unmarried couples do not embrace Christian values as they relate to marriage, but perhaps they follow these examples in society not just to be rebellious, but because they have not seen a solid model of Christian commitment in their own families or among their married friends.

Media (television, movies, video games, and the Internet) that create entertainment programs are mostly responsible for removing the mystery of sex, degrading women, trivializing marriage, and making light of unfaithfulness. The failure of adults directing these entertainment industries to uphold the sanctity of marriage, plus the divorce rate lodged in the 50 percent range, does not give young people role models to emulate.

In contrast to the films they see or the examples they observe through social networking or Internet websites is the truth about the joy of committing oneself to marriage. The challenge is to nurture young people in our families, in the church, and in our communities to desire the wholesomeness of a loving relationship that leads to a lifetime of marriage, sustained by a moral, virtuous lifestyle.

Can we work it out?

If you are just engaged or a newlywed, it is important to see why some marriages just do not work, despite good intentions. I once overheard a conversation between a young man and his girlfriend. They had been talking about marriage, when suddenly the young man said, "If it doesn't work out, we can always get a divorce." People do get married for the wrong reasons, but divorce should never be a carrot to dangle over a spouse who might one day fall short of his or her spouse's expectations.

People marry for innocent reasons, such as personality traits or physical characteristics, but eventually divorce for very different reasons. Joe, a tall, handsome blond, wanted to marry a tall, beautiful woman, so they could have beautiful children. He met Janice, a stewardess who fit his dream wife to a tee. Years after they married, he realized the fallacy of his decision; his wife was a shrew and a non-stop shopper. They went through a bitter divorce during which the wife tried everything in her power to ruin her husband's high profile and highly respected reputation in the business world.

Linda fell in love with Sam because he was romantic, friendly, and outgoing. It didn't take long after they were married for Linda to discover his romantic, friendly ways extended to other women.

Similarly, Karen was attracted to Carl's bright and creative mind. Although Carl was unemployed prior to their lavish wedding, he landed a great job soon after they were married. What Karen did not know about Carl was his workaholic tendencies. She expected him home at 6:00 p.m. every night; he often worked until midnight. They separated six weeks after they were married and divorced soon afterward.

These are just three examples of real couples who thought they were in love and destined for a long life together. They did not have the benefit of the virtues and morals that Christian couples develop and demonstrate to each other on a daily basis to offset challenges that often arise. The couples in these examples failed to keep their marriage intact because their love was not grounded in a spiritual life. They had not taken to heart the words of Ephesians 5:22, encouraging husbands to love their wives as Christ loves the church.

John Gottman explains his approximate 90 percent accuracy in predicting which couples will divorce, after watching and listening to their videotaped interaction for just five minutes. He offers the following signs that he uses to identify couples destined to divorce:

- The couple begins by being negative and making accusations.
- They show criticism, contempt, defensiveness, and stonewalling.
- The feeling of being overwhelmed by one partner's negativity leaves the other partner shell-shocked (flooding).

o Body language—conflict physiologically and visibly overwhelms men more than women.

o Getting a break in the cycle so flooding is prevented.

o Bad memories: rewriting the past in a more negative way when the marriage is not going well.

Points to Ponder

As a couple, do you share similar beliefs?

Do you attend church together and participate in the activities of your church?

Do you pray together on a daily basis and read the Bible for direction?

How do you plan to share household tasks (cooking, shopping, laundry, and so on)?

Do you expect your spouse to come home from work by a certain time every day? How would you handle it if he or she worked a lot of overtime or was a workaholic?

How do you plan to keep the romance in your marriage? (See Chapter 13 for some ideas.)

Do you agree with how frequent you should have sex and who should initiate it?

Do you plan to keep separate bank accounts or a joint account? Who should manage the finances? (Money is one of the top reasons that couples divorce.)

Have you decided when to have children?

If you are initially unable to have children, would you try fertility methods or adopt?

How do you feel about disciplining children? What is appropriate discipline, and what is out of bounds?

Do you think children should attend public school, private school, or be home-schooled?

How soon should children learn about religion, become involved in church activities, and pray?

How do you feel about one partner seeking employment in another location, necessitating a move?

What are your feelings about role reversal (women making more money; men staying at home, doing domestic duties, and looking after the children)?

What makes you angry? How do you handle it?

Do you take care of your body, eat right, work out, avoid excessive use of tobacco and alcohol, and not use drugs?

Do you have any health problems that might impact your relationship after you get married?

How would you handle a disaster, such as diagnosis of a terminal illness or a horrible accident or lost of your home due to natural causes (a storm, fire, etc.)?

Do you believe in forgiveness? Is there anything your partner could do that you would not forgive? Why?

"Marital love is a thing that no possession
can equal; for nothing, nothing whatever
(apart from heavenly good things)
is more precious than to be loved by a wife
and to love her."

St. John Chrysostom

7

A COMPELLING COVENANT

"I will betroth you to Me forever;
Yes, I will betroth you to Me
In righteousness and justice,
In lovingkindness and mercy;
I will betroth you to Me in faithfulness,
And you shall know the LORD."
Hosea 2:19-20 NKJV

By definition, a covenant is a binding agreement. From the Christian perspective, a covenant is a solemn agreement between members of the church to act together in harmony with the precepts of the Gospel.

A marriage covenant is the promise of a man and woman to become one, symbolized with a ring that serves as a constant reminder of their solemn and binding agreement, and is sealed before witnesses. A marriage before God is considered irrevocable; it is intended for a lifetime. At the heart of the covenant is a promise to remain committed and faithful, with a primary obligation of fidelity. For those called to the sacrament of marriage, it is for their mutual salvation.

Father Aimilianos underlines the importance of salvation as the finishing line, the goal and aim, of married life.

> "For many people, marriage is an opportunity for pleasures and amusements. Life, however, is a serious affair. It is a spiritual struggle, a progression toward a goal: heaven. The most crucial juncture, and the most important means of this progression, is marriage."

According to Bishop Ware, God blessed the first family of Adam and Eve and ordered them to be fruitful and multiply.

"...the Church today gives its blessing to the union of man and woman. Marriage is not only a state of nature but a state of grace. Married life...is a special vocation, requiring a particular gift or charisma from the Holy Spirit; and this gift is conferred in the sacrament of Holy Matrimony."

The partners in a covenant are responsible to each other to nurture their relationship, growing as they build up one another in love. In order to be successful, each partner has to value the other more. Jeff, who has been married for twenty-six years, offers:

"If you perceive that your spouse loves you more, you feel immeasurable value. The rare perfect marriage is when each person feels they are loved more than they love. The negative growth marriage is one in which each person feels they love more than they are loved."

Normally when we give someone a gift, it has not been requested. That is true with unconditional love in a completely committed marriage; neither partner has to ask for their gift of love. It is given freely, and it also challenges the receiver to respond by being more loving and lovable.

When a bride is ready to walk down the aisle to marry her beloved, I tell her, "If you think he is the one who is going to make you happy, you had better turn around." Happiness comes when both partners fill each other's cup, but if one is always giving, serving, and sacrificing, and the other partner is a stone wall, then the giving one gets burned.

In a recent wedding, I shared these words with the bride and groom:

> Keep in your mind, heart, and soul that you are made in the divine image and likeness of God. Be mindful of each other's needs. It is there where love will be born again and again.
>
> Happiness comes when you remind each other that marriage is holy and to be content in whatever life gives you, because it is a great mystery.
>
> Meet each other as lovers, as best friends, as companions on the journey of life, and this mystery of love will unveil itself in bits and pieces with a kind word or loving gesture.
>
> Compete only in virtues. The virtues of Christ and His Holy Church are in you. Compete by who can forgive more, who serves more, who sacrifices more, or who overlooks the insignificant issues more. This will be the engine that will take you to a higher mountain and a greater summit.
>
> Remember, you are a reflection of those who came before you, cried for you, guided you, inspired you, and prayed for you. They are the ones who gave you the wind beneath your wings. Do not withhold your gifts or talents that God has given you but give all to the service of others, your church, and your family.

A marriage surely succeeds when you are reminded daily that you have to work on it. Every day when you wake up, you must offer your gift to your relationship. For the relationship to succeed, it has to be balanced, as Jeff said. Couples who make a permanent commitment know that it requires daily work and daily sacrifice. Some sacrifices are quite simple such as giving up an event to spend special quiet time with your spouse. Considerate acts freely given to each other keep the marriage alive and lively.

As Wadell says, we are made for community, a community of love that can be expressed only when love is offered to the other and it is returned. In fact, when the partners in a Christian covenant experience the unconditional love of Christ, they love each other the same way. Beyond showing unconditional love to one another, they demonstrate forgiveness and reconciliation. The foundation of the covenant is selfless love, freely given and freely received.

St. Paul said in 1 Corinthians 13:8, "Love never fails." Love is the tie that binds a couple together for the remainder of their time on Earth. When we know that our lives are forever tied together, we act differently. In our covenant, we have promised to stay with each other and work through our troubles "till death us do part."

Understanding the true significance of marriage as a sacrament is one of the most important steps in preparing for married life. It is not an exchange of vows before God, family, and friends; in fact, in some faiths, such as the Orthodox Christian faith, the couple does not exchange vows during the wedding. They are building a foundation that will support their marriage "for better" and "for worse." They live with the knowledge that God united them in holy matrimony and will not let them go. Of course, only with couples who share a common faith in God can this covenant work. Their common faith gives them the courage to believe in God's everlasting love and presence in their lives.

What was hidden in the Old Testament became revealed in the New Testament. On several occasions in the New Testament, Christ quotes the Old Testament, that from the beginning it was God's intention to make us love, and for marriage to be whole and wholesome. But you ask, "What about when people do not get along and break up?" In a very profound statement, which I am paraphrasing from Matthew 19, Jesus said because they are hard in their hearts, and when they are hard in their hearts, there will be no reconciliation. They've already made up their minds.

Wedding vows

The exchange of wedding vows by the bride and groom is an approach which indicates the couple's consent to make their decision to wed. In the original tradition of the church, however, Christ united the couple, but the couple was required to have good intention, which is measured by the way they live up to their

> Couples today speak of love for the here and now but not for eternity.

promises. When we reflect that a higher authority invites us to the sacrament of marriage, we do not take it as lightly as we take our own promises. Many times we make promises and then we break them. In churches where couples write their own vows, they go from the most sensitive to the most outrageous. What is lost in these vows is the meaning of commitment.

Vows should reflect the couple's love inspired by God, their commitment inspired by the Church, and their faithfulness inspired by the fidelity to one another. Life will take you places you have never dreamt. Even if you do not go anywhere, love might take you through sickness or another crisis. This love comes from God, and we are to reflect that love by being patient, being kind, by not being contemptuous or critical, by not stonewalling.

With almost half of all marriages ending in divorce, maybe we are not as perfect as we think we are. The intention is honorable, but, as they say, the road to hell is paved with good intentions. Good intention is not enough; it is the journey that will take you through life that will help you fulfill these vows. When you start out, you really don't have the experience, so these vows will become stronger through crisis and tribulation, through disagreements and dialogue.

In fact, in the Orthodox Church, part of the service blesses the promises the couple has made during courtship and engagement. They are to take a lifelong journey to fulfill them. Too often, the marriage vows are spoken with finality, when they really should mark the beginning of the couple's commitment.

> O Lord our God, bless the betrothal of these thy servants (names) and confirm the word which they have spoken. Establish them in the holy union which is from thee. For thou, in the beginning, didst make them male and female, and by thee is the woman joined unto the man as a helpmeet. Wherefore, O Lord our God, who has sent forth thy truth upon thine inheritance, and thy covenant unto thy servants our fathers, even thine elect, from generation to generation: Look thou upon thy servant (name) and upon thy handmaid (name) and establish their betrothal in faith and in oneness of mind, in truth and in love. *Orthodox Wedding Prayer*

Personalizing marriage vows affords the couple the opportunity to express their heartfelt feelings and intentions. With all of the other details that require the couple's attention, the personalized vows should not be written in a last-minute rush. Allow plenty of time (at least a month) to prepare the first draft, review it, rewrite it, set it aside, and re-read it at a later date. Sometimes in a later reading, the need for changes will become apparent. Vows can be identical, or they can be similar or very different, but the couple should read each other's vows before the wedding, so there are no surprises that might spoil the occasion. (It has been known to happen!)

Even if the couple opts to write their own vows, they might find that reading samples of traditional vows will inspire them or give them meaningful ideas for their own vows. Other sources of inspiration are songs, poetry, sermons, the Bible, and quotes from books that mean something special.

If the couple is being married in a church, they should make sure their vows are appropriate for the setting and for the commitment they are making. Even in a non-church setting, such as on a beach or mountaintop or in a special hall, the vows should reflect the couple's intentions, the seriousness of the occasion, and the commitment they are making. Sometimes humor or poetry can be incorporated, as long as it is appropriate for the occasion and location.

It is advisable that each individual vow be limited to about a minute, and for the bride and groom to practice reading their vows ahead of the ceremony to make their official exchange seem more natural.

Points to Ponder

What is a covenant?

What does a covenant mean in marriage?

Is a covenant binding? If so, how is it binding?

What is at the heart of a covenant of marriage?

How does one prepare to enter into a covenant of marriage?

What is the foundation of Christian love?

Do you prefer traditional vows or personalized ones?

If you already wrote or are thinking about writing your own vows, why?

What should be at the core of personalized vows?

Have you taken up the meaningful habit of writing to each other after getting married?

8

POST-WEDDING ADJUSTMENTS

"There is hardly any activity,
any enterprise, which is started
with such tremendous hopes and expectations
and which fails so regularly as love."
Erich Fromm

Following the wedding and the wedding night, most couples go away for a honeymoon. In the first place, we have the wrong definition to the honeymoon. Many people think that it is a fantasy, an exotic and unrealistic sexual escapade. They don't realize that fierce passions tend to calm down to a different kind of passion, so the honeymoon will be viewed one day as the beginning of their becoming soul mates. People think it is magical. It is not magical. It is a coming together, a merger.

Keeping that spark alive takes healthy communication, which means dialogue, not monologue. Here is a helpful checklist to clarify the meaning of good dialogue:

- Love is the spark that ignites the flame of dialogue.
- Each speaker is open to the needs of the other.
- Communication is a two-sided exchange.
- The subject matter is discussed honestly.
- The dialogue participants respect each other.
- Listening is the most effective form of communication.
- Communication goes through constant changes.
- Communication fosters the courage for emotional growth.
- Dialogue produces harmony.
- In dialogue, no one is defined by himself or herself, but they communicate with one another and with God.

Dialogue is not just about expressing feelings. Sometimes we express them in the wrong place and at the wrong time for the wrong reasons; that might produce abuse and hostility and deeply hurt feelings. Healthy dialogue is about resolving issues that crop up daily instead of letting them fester for months or years. If you become good at addressing your conflicts, you forgive in time and that leads to intimacy. This is how people move from the honeymoon to a relationship that will outlive their daily disagreements.

So the honeymoon means that instead of riding the locomotive and going 100 mph, you move to another compartment of the train, but the train keeps going. You can still enjoy the scenery, but it will be different scenery over different seasons.

Aside from the honeymoon, there is also a lot of fantasy about love and romance and living happily ever after. One day a lady came to me after being married just a short time. She said, "I think my husband and I are falling out of love."

"What happened?" I asked her.

"We had a disagreement. We fought for the first time," she said candidly.

"Congratulations," I said. "You found love."

"What do you mean, we found love?" she asked.

"Love demands that you do your best," I said.

I always encourage young married couples to be patient. They have to go through a period of adjustment. Sometimes, one family or another will interfere and move the newlyweds off track. Disagreements that were hidden before the wedding usually surface either the night of the wedding or after the wedding, because couples lean back on their families. I instruct them so, "You each came from different families, but now you have to make your own family."

After the honeymoon, the couple should realize they are human beings; they are not perfect. If they take into consideration each other first, they will always be mindful of their spouse. We do not go to school to learn how to be a couple, but if a couple has the foundation of a healthy perspective on life and the mutuality of respect and faith, these will help them along the journey. In the United States, we have lost the virtue of surviving, the coping mechanism. The minute we reach a dead end, we lose hope. We think it is over. We have become so independent that we have lost the ability to extend ourselves and ask for help.

Coping comes by faith. Journeys involve taking time, patience, commitment, and endurance. In our society, television news, Facebook, and Twitter offer immediate answers instead of saying, "Let us figure it out." We still have time. Endurance teaches us to be strong, to reach out to one another, and look at the bigger picture and not settle for an instant digital snapshot.

After the wedding and honeymoon are over, the married couple faces the realities of married life—making large and small decisions, being sensitive to each other's daily needs, learning

> "Marriage is not a life-long love affair; it is an ordeal."
> *Joseph Campbell*

to be *dependent* after years of being *independent*, building and settling a home, and establishing day-in and day-out routines. The lifestyle changes are enormous, especially if the couple has known each other and dated for only a year or two. Even those who have grown up together or dated for ten years will face adjustments after they get married.

Time management can be a very difficult adjustment when you first get married, because instead of managing just your own time, you suddenly have to keep track of your spouse's, scheduling classes (if you are still in school), making time for in-laws and other family members, and making sure there is enough day left for some private time for you as a couple. This is often where sacrifice enters the picture. If spending more time with your spouse means you give up working out or attending a cooking class, then opt for spending more time with your spouse. In the long run, the sacrifice will be worth it.

The adventure of mutual discovery is another challenging adjustment to newlyweds. ("Oldlyweds" might still be struggling in this area too.) Like our good friends who help us see ourselves in a different, hopefully better light, we also wake up to these discoveries as newlyweds. In a good marriage, husband and wife share their burdens and weaknesses along with their dreams and strengths without being concerned about how the other person will react to them.

It might be tempting to think you are going to change the person you married, but that is a serious misconception. One elderly woman who knows from experience has this advice for young women: "Don't marry a man to reform him." Of course, it goes both ways. Men should not marry a woman to change her. What both can hope for is that in time and by their example, the spouse will grow and abandon some of the quirks in behavior that are irritable or completely undesirable.

As we already have discussed in this book, the best way to encourage change and growth in our beloved is to concentrate on being the best we can be, to correct our own shortcomings, to forgive, and to love as Christ loves each of us, faults and all.

Flying an airplane takes a lot of experience—learning the significance of myriad buttons and dials in the cockpit, practicing take-off and landing maneuvers, and knowing how to recognize brewing storms. Marriage is similar, but one thing is certain: There is no automatic pilot when it comes to making marriage successful. To keep a marriage aloft, partners must make a commitment. The Protestant and Catholic vows say, "for better, for worse, for richer, for poorer, in sickness and in health, forsaking all others, so long as we both shall live." That expresses a covenant, a lifetime commitment, through every conceivable circumstance the couple will face in marriage.

Getting off on the right foot

Successfully married couples often admit that they married their best friends. Being best friends and lovers serves as a good foundation for marriage, but it requires constant work. Having a best friend means being a best friend, and we've already learned that in order to be that, we must love ourselves first. By acting in loving ways, we create loving feelings in our partner.

> A successful marriage is marrying someone with whom you enjoy doing *nothing*.

A man wanted a divorce because he no longer loved his wife. He happened to live in a state that required a six-month waiting period before he could file divorce papers. Being a reasonable man, he decided to make lemonade with the lemons he had been given. He made a list of all the things he would do if he loved his wife, and then he started to do these things. By the end of his six-month waiting period, he had fallen madly in love with the woman he could not wait to leave a few months earlier. He learned the value of giving and receiving love.

How do couples succeed at being friends and lovers? They spend time enjoying each other.

They schedule dates just like they did before they married. They always greet each other with affection. And lastly, they give each other pleasure in innumerable ways every day.

When a couple can add to each other's happiness and perceive what healthy happiness is, they become happier, instead of saying "We have more than enough food, yet we are hungry. We have more than enough military might, yet we feel insecure. We have the greatest jobs and more than enough money, yet we feel lonely." Why would two career-driven executives as husband and wife come home and feel lonely?

Happiness happens only when you reach out to others, not only to make yourself happy, but also to share goodness with them. That gives you the energy to keep going. In marriage, happiness must be reciprocated.

Short learning curve

Statistics show that couples are the most vulnerable in the first three years of their marriage, and most divorces occur in the first five years. These alarming statistics, with an overall divorce rate still hovering at 50 percent, underscore the importance of learning everything possible to ensure a successful marriage.

Post-wedding adjustments include the wake-up call to discover imperfections in the spouse we once thought was perfect, just like we expected our world to be perfectly wonderful once we were married. Bliss is just around the corner, or so we hoped.

Because we often enter into marriage with unrealistic expectations, we must work even harder to learn to talk to our spouse openly, expressing how we feel, think, and believe. We also have to be equally willing to listen to our spouse's expressions of feelings, thoughts, and beliefs. Most of us are not mind readers. Some individuals do not know how to open up or they are concerned their spouse might not understand or appreciate how they think or feel or believe about something. Holding back is not the answer, however. The more we know our partner before marriage, the less likely we will receive major surprises, but talking and listening will always be necessary in marriage.

Listening to our spouse requires empathy. What message is he or she saying "between the lines"? We have to learn to listen not only to the spoken words, but to the unspoken thoughts that are sometime difficult to put into words. The unspoken message might well be an unmet emotional need (affection, attention or more time alone). If the underlying message is critical but the spouse cannot articulate his or her thoughts, the listening spouse needs to refrain from reacting defensively but instead should learn to react in such a way as to show an effort to understand their spouse's reason for criticizing and to enter meaningful dialogue to keep the criticism from escalating into an argument.

If both spouses had a particularly difficult day— maybe the husband at work and the wife managing the household—both need to allow time for the other to vent their frustrations. Each partner deserves to feel heard, but they both benefit if they take turns spilling out their anger or irritations before moving on. This requires patience for one spouse, which might help the other spouse cool off and put his or her aggravations into perspective.

A critical part of communication that is lacking in today's marriages is praise. It need not be lavish; it can be as simple as a kiss or an "I love you." Everyone wants to be praised and appreciated, even when he or she has not done anything special or achieved anything particularly noteworthy. When couples marry their best friends, praise comes easily, but busy couples sometimes forget or get too bogged down in their busy lives. Nurturing marriage with praise helps to keep it on solid footing.

We communicate during the day easily enough with cell phones and social networking avenues, but for the married couple, in the quiet of their room before going to sleep, some of the most romantic and heartwarming communication comes by way of "pillow talk." That kind of intimacy creates a deep bond.

Outside influences

For newlyweds who are struggling or at least coping with adjustments to married life, it might serve them well to spend time with other newlyweds. In fact, one study at Wayne State University two years ago showed that establishing friendships with other newlyweds strengthens a couple's relationship, reinforces their own sense of togetherness, and makes them feel closer to each other.

> "Pillow talk" is more important than sex.

On the other hand, nothing undermines a new marriage more than complaining to family and friends about one's spouse. Even if the complaints are expressed in confidence, sooner or later, the spouse will find out. Personal complaints should be expressed to each other in the marriage and ironed out, unless the partners reach an impasse and mutually decide to seek outside intervention.

The couple's families have a sacred duty to help the newlyweds get over any difficult adjustments to starting a life together by lending a hand, by being there, by offering support but not by imposing on them.

One outside influence that works against marital success is not a person; it is the past of each spouse. Whatever happened to each one, romantically or otherwise, or between the couple before they got married (a major argument, for instance) needs to be released to the past where it belongs. Holding on to grudges prevents the couple from focusing on their marriage in the here and now.

Growing and growing up

We've touched on growing pains in relationships, but for a good marriage to succeed, each partner needs to let go of immaturity, give up childish ways, and grow up. One man started out on the wrong foot on his wedding night by bringing a Frisbee to the bridal suite! Having fun is one thing, but being immature, irresponsible, throwing temper tantrums, being jealous, and demanding one's own way are surefire ways to bring marriage to a screeching halt.

An important component of mature people is forgiveness. We will delve more deeply into this virtue in Chapter 12. Both partners must be willing to forgive each other every day. By constantly asking forgiveness, we offset the likelihood of feelings getting hurt, of growing apart, and of wounds not getting healed. God blesses the husband and wife, who forgive each other, as Christ has repeatedly taught us to do.

The happiest couples act toward each other out of loving kindness by treating each other like best friends. This is another sign of maturity in a marital relationship (or in any relationship). In addition, research reports that couples who enter into deep, substantive conversations with each other are measurably happier than those who dwell on small talk.

Sharing affection and engaging in sex should be the most enjoyable part of married life, but even those exciting elements can get lost in the shuffle of everyday adjustments and shared routines. The best way to start a day is with a hug and a kiss and an "I love you." If you can't do it when you greet the day, make sure that before it is over, you connect with one another this way. It is definitely a great (and enjoyable) way to secure your bond with your spouse.

Studies show that men crave feeling special and being noticed by their wives, and the men who report not getting enough nonsexual affection were twice as likely to seek a divorce. For women, that is not the case. They absorb affection and affirmation from mothers, children, or best girlfriends, so some women may need less affection from their husbands. Making sure your husband receives regular cuddling, kissing, and other tokens of your love and affection will keep him happy.

Hints for a happy marriage

These helpful hints will encourage any couple to build (or rebuild) a marriage in which both know when to talk and when to listen:

- When you must choose between making yourself or your spouse look good, choose your spouse.
- Always share affectionate greetings.
- Express criticism as lovingly as possible.
- Use self-discipline to yield to the other's wishes.
- Take turns being angry.
- Reserve yelling for emergencies or sports games.
- Leave past mistakes in the past; they serve no purpose now.

- Practice putting each other first.

- When one spouse errs, he or she should talk to the other about it and ask forgiveness.

- In a quarrel, remember that the one who does the most talking makes the least sense.

- Always make peace before going to bed.

- End each day with a kind word or compliment.

Points to Ponder

What did you expect everyday married life to be like?

How have your expectations about everyday married life changed since you got married?

After the wedding, what was the first thing that bothered you about your spouse?

What was the first thing that bothered your spouse about you?

How does each of you deal with pet peeves, petty annoyances, and little irritations in one another?

How have you changed to minimize the annoyance caused by your pet peeves? (Picked up your clothes, rinsed your dirty dishes, etc.)

What is the most difficult behavior or attitude in your spouse that you have had to accept?

What is the most difficult behavior or attitude in you that your spouse has had to accept?

When did you last learn something new about your spouse?

When did your spouse last learn something new about you?

How do you celebrate anniversaries (first kiss, first date, etc.)?

When was the last time you planned a special, romantic dinner either at home or away for just the two of you?

Do you and your spouse practice loving pillow talk?

Do you and your spouse make the master bedroom off-limits to everything but sleeping, sex, and loving "pillow talk"?

9

MONEY & MARRIAGE

"In marriage, be wise: prefer the person before money,
virtue before beauty, the mind before the body;
then thou hast a wife, a friend, a companion, and a second self."
William Penn
English philosopher & founder of Pennsylvania

Money and all financial topics cause more arguments, serious conflicts, and divorce than any other issue that married couples face. In Hebrews 13:5, it says:

"Let your conversation be without covetness; and be content with such things as ye have: for he hath said, I will never leave thee or forsake thee."

Money and the management of money are an important part of our daily lives.

Despite the time-worn saying that money is the root of all evil, people don't fight over money itself; they fight over its meaning. How important is money to the couple? Is one more materialistic than the other? Does one run up credit card debts easily? Does the couple believe it is important to start saving early for retirement many years down the road?

Whether the newlyweds are young and just getting started earning incomes or an older couple already established in their careers, money presents different avenues to conflict. The younger couple might be naïve and inexperienced in managing money, credit, and investments. The more mature couple, just newly married, might have problems converting from independent management of finances to joint considerations in that department.

Couples who do not know how to communicate about money (or other matters) often resort to using money to punish or hold hostage. A man who controls the money, largely because of a single-income situation, might keep his spouse on a tight leash, doling out what amounts to an allowance, barely sufficient to meet the household expenses she must manage. Women today find themselves in a similar position if they are the principal breadwinner.

In the age of online dating, today's couples first want to know the other person's credit score. That is a positive step in the right direction. The sooner a couple discusses money and finances, the better they will be able to handle money ups and downs as their relationship progresses, even to marriage.

In order to keep the lines of communication about money and finances open, they need to adopt a communication model based on dialogue, on give-and-take conversation. (See Chapter 8 for more about dialogue.) Dialogue makes the discussion of money easier when it comes to planning and budgeting. A responsible approach to money management in marriage means that the money issue will less likely be the center of conflict.

The fact that marriage indeed is a partnership means that both partners need to be involved in all issues—especially money and finances—that arise in day-to-day living. Perhaps the most obvious step for newlyweds is to start planning their budget together. Put all the cards (income, expenses, and debts) on the table and plot out a monthly budget to determine how to allocate the single or joint income. From time to time, it is important to sit down and review the family budget to see what adjustments might be in order.

Experts in finances and relationships suggest that from the beginning, couples should pool their money, in part to prevent one partner from exercising too much power over the other, but also to institute transparency in financial matters.

It is also important for couples to adopt a plan to each have separate checking accounts and credit cards to give them a greater sense of autonomy as well as empowerment to take responsibility for their own finances. For the spouse who does not work but relies on the other to provide the family income, having separate checking accounts and credit cards enables them both to establish good credit, should some calamity interrupt the main source of income in the family.

In the days before credit cards became so prevalent, families lived virtually debt-free. If they didn't have the cash to purchase something, they did without it. Couples today should adopt that debt-free lifestyle. Paying off credit cards in full each month will prevent runaway debt problems later on.

Along the same line, experts recommend that couples discuss how to handle major purchases, such as an automobile, furniture, and vacations. Select a certain amount which can be discretionary purchases by either spouse, agreeing that any purchases over that amount requires dialogue between the spouses. Having an agreement like this provides a sense of accountability.

If both spouses are earning money to support the family, before and after children arrive, they need to continue working to build reserves in the event that one spouse loses his or her job or a serious illness derails the breadwinner. If income goes down, remember to cut back on spending to stay on budget to the best of your ability.

Money problems in marriage arise late in life too. I have heard from more than one widow that her husband, who had handled all of their financial affairs, left their finances in disarray. One woman told me that she did not know her husband had a life insurance policy where he worked. She found out accidentally after he passed. The message is clear: if one spouse handles the family's major financial concerns, he or she must leave an up-to-date accounting of all money matters for the surviving spouse.

Points to Ponder

Were you each totally honest about your individual financial situation before marriage?

Was either of you in debt before marriage? If so, what plan did you have for getting out of debt?

Did you—or will you—take a couple's money management course?

As a couple, are your ideas about spending—and saving—compatible?

Do you share the importance of long-term saving (for retirement)?

Who will—or does—handle investments?

Do you believe in separate checking accounts? Savings?

If only one person works, how will money be allocated to the non-working partner?

Who handles—or will handle—payment of monthly bills?

How do you feel about prenuptial agreements? Would you sign one if your partner asked you to do so?

10

GRACE UNDER PRESSURE

*"When we long for life without difficulties,
remind us that oaks grow strong in contrary winds
and diamonds are made under pressure."*
Rev. Peter Marshall

Even with discovering, adjusting, managing time, setting up a home, and juggling one another's schedules, there are many other pressures in a marriage. A married couple faces peer and societal pressure about how they should look and conduct themselves in public (should they conform or not?); parental hints about starting a family; attitudes toward money, keeping up with the Joneses, and moving up the career ladder; and most recently, acceptance or rejection of role reversal options.

Pressure, as we read in Rev. Peter Marshall's opening quote to this chapter, can be healthy. It helps us become better people as we strive to reach our highest potential. Pressure becomes a threat to our lives or marriage is when it grows out of proportion to our ability to handle it. It might also be affected by the age and emotional maturity of the couple. Young couples might not have acquired the coping mechanism to handle the decisions necessary for managing pressure. Most stress in marriage is normal, but if the couple cannot navigate pressures and the decisions that go with them, they should seek outside help. To field any number of pressures takes grace, and grace requires focus and control.

Practicing grace under pressure helps us to lead by example, showing others how to behave under trying circumstances. We should act the way we would want others around us to act.

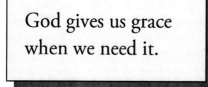

God gives us grace
when we need it.

If we do not think of ourselves as a role model yet, we can choose someone who has been a role model for us, and let that person inspire us as to how we should act in tough situations.

We must reassure ourselves that we have what it takes. We keep cool under pressure better when we think positively.

Refocus the problem (and the pressure it is causing us) to brainstorm ways to solve the problem. Exercise grace in the efforts you use to make the situation better. And while directing your focus away from the problem, look at it as one small incident in life. If you view the big picture, you will find it easier to be graceful.

Dr. Wayne Dyer offers a technique that helps us minimize the pressures of our daily life. If a particular situation is causing stress, find a peaceful, quiet place (even before falling asleep at night) and imagine you are hovering over Earth, getting a bird's eye-view of the tragedies, calamities, and heartbreaks far beyond anything you are enduring. Somehow, suddenly, the problem pales by comparison.

Our perspective on our problems is critical. Once we alter that perspective, we can proceed with renewed grace. Daily prayer also offers relief from stress and renews our ability to carry on, even in the face of life's great challenges. Prayer offers us the opportunity to remove our cares and worries from our own hands, instead entrusting them to God's hands.

St. Gennadius of Constantinople instructs us to give our concerns:

"...in prayer to God, Who knows everyone, even before our birth. And do not ask that everything will be according to your will, because a man does not know what is profitable for him. But say to God: Let Thy will be done! For he does everything for our benefit."

Another technique is to imagine a worst- and best-case scenario. Fear of the worst redirects our focus and can lead to failure. If we imagine the worst, our imagination might help us to develop ways to offset failure or create a back-up plan if the worst does come.

Admittedly it is more enjoyable to imagine best-case scenarios—writing a bestseller, getting a promotion at work, or winning mega millions in the lottery. Thinking about successful outcomes triggers the brain to tell us how we can realize them.

The inevitability of stress

For newlyweds, stress is inevitable, as it is in every human relationship. Jesus said that when two or three are gathered together, He would be in their midst (Matthew 18:20). But when two get together, stress happens. Stress can come from outside the home or it can be generated without any outside influence. Stress can come from family, career, financial concerns, and also from inner conflicts such as personality clashes or an abusive relationship. In married life, as happy as the couple is when their first child arrives, it comes with stress. Learning how to deal with a toddler's temper tantrums and cope with teenagers' changing moods can be very stressful for a couple.

Stress is inevitable, but in marriage a couple makes promises to one another, and if they cannot find solutions from within, there is always counseling or family support. The worst stress comes with the death of a child or family member, but it can make the couple stronger, too, if their relationship has been built on a strong foundation. If not, any cause of stress will rock the ship and even capsize it.

One frequent cause of divorce is the inability to deal with the catastrophic illness of a spouse. That is the new weakness in today's families: the lack of commitment when facing dire situations. People are too consumed with their own needs and individualism. They do not take into account other people

> In times of crisis, we either melt down or we rise to the occasion.

in their life. "My wife needs a mastectomy, but I'm out of here. I married a woman with two breasts and now she will have only one." Or if the husband is diagnosed with prostate cancer, the wife might believe that the marriage is over.

Some people in difficult circumstances still face each new day very happy and satisfied with their romantic life, their intimate life, and their sexual life. This is where our best comes out.

Seven-year itch

There is always an itch in marriage, but it should not derail the train. In everyday life, we face obstacles. All of our flaws surface after about four or five years, but what complicates it is not knowing that after seven years, we are moving from stage one to stage two to stage three in the relationship. The first seven to ten years are the most difficult to deal with as a couple, but they have to deal with challenges in later years and in empty-nest marriages too.

The seven-year itch legitimizes our lack of courage to understand that we should have grown, we should have had patience. When we are afraid to grow, we become stuck. No trees remain in the same shape, but we know that the trees we plant are growing roots, and the deeper the roots, the stronger the trees and their ability to withstand the storms that come their way. The same is true with the foundation of a relationship and how the strength of that foundation helps it to survive.

People forget that marriage requires work, and love is not enough. An elderly woman by the name of Irene gave me an embroidered motto: A PEACEFUL AND CONFIDENT HOME IS PART OF HEAVEN, A PARADISE. What does that say? You cannot generate peace by wishing for it. You cannot desire confidence by wishing for it.

> Flowers remind us to be kind.

The couple's first priority is to remember that their home is a paradise, and to have a paradise, they must bring virtues. Create peace. Consider the other. Forgive one another. Remind each other of the virtues that maintain a good home. Ask what you are bringing home. Do you bring stress or do you bring flowers?

Stress-busters

A variety of stress-busting technique will help you to refocus your attention and give yourself the grace to solve whatever pressures are building in your life. 1) Select a favorite Scripture verse to repeat regularly. Philippians 4:13 is a good one to keep in mind: "I can do all things through Christ which strengtheneth me." 2) When you are under pressure, make a list of priorities you can do to relieve pressure. 3) Listen to relaxing, soothing music. 4) Realize that you cannot change the past or predict the future; take life one day at a time. 5) Laugh. Laughter is great medicine. 6) Sit on a beach or by a brook; naturally running water is soothing. 7) Be courageous. Ernest Hemingway said, "Courage is grace under pressure." 8) When all else fails, pretend. Act like you think someone you admire would act in your situation. 9) Pray and seek spiritual support from someone you respect, such as your pastor or another esteemed church member.

> God, give us the grace to accept with serenity
> The things that cannot be changed,
> The courage to change the things
> Which should be changed,
> And the wisdom to distinguish
> One from the other.
>
> *Reinhold Niebuhr*

Points to Ponder

Are you easily stressed out?

What are your most common causes of stress?

When you are stressed, do you act like a role model or seek a role model to emulate in a given stressful situation?

What is grace? How do you get it? How do you use it?

What are your best ways to handle stress?

Would you seek outside intervention to help you handle stress?

Do you consider your home a paradise? If so, what makes it a paradise? If not, how can you make it more like one?

How do you maintain peace in your home environment?

11

THE CULTURE OF
CLOSENESS AND CONFLICT

"For a marriage to have any chance,
Every day at least six things should go unsaid."
Author unknown

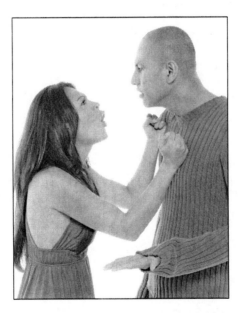

Wherever a couple lives or works, or how much money they have,

some day one of them will disagree, and the other one will react.

Then one thing leads to another, and suddenly there is a bigger problem to resolve. It is all part of our daily communication, but normal dialogue between mates is calm and controlled, not argumentative. One or both partners usually get hurt during a confrontation over something trivial or more serious.

> "Many marriages would be better if
> the husband and wife clearly understood
> that they are on the same side."
> *Zig Ziglar*

Most marital arguments cannot be resolved, according to John Gottman, because most of their disagreements are lodged in differences, when the real cause of any argument in and out of marriage is misunderstanding. To prevent quarreling and hostility, we need to address this issue.

John Gottman's new model for resolving conflict in a marriage suggests the following steps: 1) soften the start-up (tiptoe into the problem), 2) learn to make and receive repair attempts, 3) be soothing to each other, 4) compromise, and 5) tolerate each other's faults.

In most marriages, women are more likely to open up a touchy subject than men, but women can run the gamut from being sweet to sarcastic. The one who tiptoes into the problem avoids the galloping four horsemen of conflict, but the one who starts out with sarcasm invites all four of them into the dispute.

To start-up softly, Gottman recommends that the couple complain but not blame, start statements with "I" instead of "You," describe what is happening without evaluating or judging, be clear, be polite, be appreciative, and not store things up or let them fester over time. "Be ye angry, and sin not: let not the sun go down upon your wrath." *Ephesians 4:26*

A repair attempt tones down the tension so that the other partner becomes more willing to find a compromise. Repair attempts do not have to be extremely skillful; they just need to get through to the other partner. When that partner makes a repair attempt, it is important for the other partner to accept it.

Attempts to soothe each other are important to avoid flooding (becoming overwhelmed emotionally and physically). Gottman notes that in most cases where one spouse does not embrace the other's repair attempt, it is because the listening spouse is flooded and cannot hear what the other spouse is saying. If your heart rate exceeds a hundred beats per minute, you will not be able to hear what your spouse is trying to tell you, no matter how hard you try. Take a twenty-minute break before you continue.

Soothing the other partner is greatly beneficial to the marriage. If one partner is frequently being calmed by the other, the first one will associate that partner with relaxation, not with stress.

Compromise is the only solution to marital problems. For a compromise to work, one partner cannot have a closed mind to the other partner's opinions and wishes. There must be honest openness to considering the other person's position. They must be willing to accept influence from their spouse. Men typically find it more difficult to accept influence from their wives. If they cannot be open-minded, it is a liability to successful conflict resolution.

Responsibility also lies with the wife to present her position or request in a loving manner, to use her influence for the improvement of her spouse and not for selfish gains. When open-mindedness, and, yes, even self-sacrifice, is met with love, great harmony of compromise can flourish in married life.

St. John Chrysostom, in his Homily on St. John, describes the beautiful balance of a wife's loving influence on her husband:

> "Nothing is more powerful than a pious and sensible woman to bring her husband into proper order, and to mold his soul as she wills. For he will not listen to friends, or teachers, or rulers, as much as he will his partner advising and counseling him, since the advice carries some pleasures with it, because she who gives the counsel is greatly loved.

I could tell of many hard and disobedient men who have been softened this way. For she who shares his table, his bed, and his embraces, his words and secrets, his comings in and goings out, and many other things, who is entirely given up and joined to him, as it is likely that a body would be joined to a head, if she happens to be discreet and well attuned, will go beyond and excel all others in the management of her husband."

Finally, a couple needs to be tolerant of each other's faults and flaws. As long as they remain intolerant, they cannot reach a successful compromise.

Four horsemen

John Gottman's four horsemen of conflict in relationships do not appear in a specific order. The first horseman is criticism. Criticism is the blame game of conflict. When couples employ negative words about each other's personality, that leads to character assassination. Asking a question such as "What's wrong with you?" simply adds more fuel to the fire.

Criticism is very common in relationships. The first sign of criticism should not sound an alarm that the marriage is doomed. But if it becomes persistent, it opens the gate for the other deadly horsemen.

The second horseman in conflict is contempt which includes name-calling, sarcasm, eye-rolling, sneering, mockery, and hostile humor. In any of those forms, contempt is toxic to a relationship because the underlying feeling is one of disgust, which turns off any attempt to resolve the conflict. Inevitably contempt leads to more conflict instead of reconciliation.

Long-lasting negative thoughts that simmer under the surface fuel contempt. Partners with unresolved differences are more likely to entertain these thoughts. (An interesting aside is that couples who express contempt for one another are more likely to develop health problems like colds and flu than other people.)

The third horseman is defensiveness or blaming one's partner. "This escalates the problem, which is why it's so deadly," Gottman explains.

Criticism, contempt, and defensiveness do not always appear in a strict order. They function like a relay match, in which one hands off a baton to another over and over again if the couple cannot stop them.

Discussions that begin with a harsh start-up, criticism, contempt, and defensiveness can lead one partner to tune out. And this allows entry of the fourth horseman—stonewalling.

In ordinary conversations, we can tell when the other party is listening and paying attention. With their body language primarily or an occasional word of acknowledgment, the person indicates that they are following what the other person is saying. The one who stonewalls, on the other hand, looks away, remains silent, and just sits like, well, a stone wall. Even if he hears, he doesn't really care what the other is saying.

Stonewalling, which is used as a last resort, is uncommon with newlyweds because they have not built up enough negativity in their marriage to utilize this horseman.

Gottman notes four stages that signal the end of a relationship:

1) Seeing your marital problems as severe
2) Talking them over seems useless; resorting to solve them on your own
3) Starting to lead separate lives, even under the same roof and
4) Feeling more and more lonely, again even while still living under the same roof.

If the couple makes it to the fourth stage, there is a greater likelihood that one of the spouses will enter into an extramarital affair.

Keeping conflict at bay

Couples that encounter problems from time to time can resolve their differences and keep them from escalating to full-blown conflicts. When an issue arises, one partner might acknowledge it and extend an olive branch of appreciation to the other partner. After stating positive things about the situation before it becomes a disagreement, the partner can state his or her position on the matter. The other person needs to repeat the concern to be sure that they heard it correctly.

As the discussion continues, they calmly exchange their thoughts and concerns and offer a compromise that is mutually acceptable to both spouses.

If the problem concerns something a spouse did wrong, he or she should apologize. It must be a sincere apology, which means the offending spouse admits to the wrongdoing, takes responsibility for his or her actions, and agrees to not do it again.

The other side of apologizing is forgiving, which we will discuss in depth in the next chapter. In an honest discussion, where one person has truly offered the carrot of apology, the injured party needs to forgive. Both "I'm sorry" and "I forgive you" are equally important. After the apology has been accepted and the party forgiven, the offense needs to be buried and never mentioned again. Too often, couples have a memory lapse in this regard and drag out the dirty laundry from the past to add fuel to any current conflict.

Differences

When you are building, maintaining, and protecting a relationship like marriage, you need to develop skills that might not be the same as those you would use in another part of your life.

It is important to understand the distinction between difference and disagreement. If you and your spouse differ without having a disagreement, these differences do not necessarily impact your decisions about where to eat out, when to vote, and what movie you should see. On the other hand, if the difference is about buying a house or moving across the country, you cannot go forward until you resolve that difference.

When you marry, you make a commitment to stay together, but if your personal space is limited (you live in a tiny newlywed apartment), each of you must tactfully negotiate your needs for socializing, usage of time, standards for tidiness and cleanliness, and other basic issues that require joint decision-making. In such circumstances, for instance, if one spouse is studying or working at home, the other spouse needs to respect his or her spouse's need for peace and quiet.

When disagreements heat up and become conflicts, your pulse rises, your breathing accelerates, and maybe you start to sweat. That is due to your body pumping adrenalin into your system because it believes danger is imminent, and it is preparing you for fight or flight. Whenever the fight instinct arises, it repels responses to compromise. When you cannot feel love for your partner, conflict occurs in a space where the caring that you normally feel for one another usually lives.

This is when you must make a choice: resolve the conflict and feel good about each other or feel resentful, making your relationship rocky for a while.

It is easier to resolve a conflict if you can step back and cool off first. This is the only way that you can resolve conflict in marriage and have you and your spouse feel heard and respected.

As St. Paul says in 2 Timothy 4:7, "I have fought the good fight, I have finished my course, I have kept the faith."

And in 1 Corinthians 9:24, we are reminded of the reward that comes with winning the race:

> "Do you know that in a race
> All the runners run,
> But only one gets the prize.
> Run in such a way as to get the prize."

16 rules for fair fighting

David H. Olson and John DeFrain have developed an excellent checklist of rules for fighting fairly, as follows:

1. Negotiate from the adult position.
2. Avoid ultimatums.
3. If one loses, both lose.
4. Say what you really mean.
5. Avoid accusations and attack.
6. Own your own feelings first.
7. Always check out your perceptions.
8. State your wishes and requests early and directly.
9. Never use sex to smooth over a disagreement
10. Repeat the message you think you received
11. Refuse to fight dirty.
12. Resist giving the silent treatment.
13. Focus on the issue and on the present.
14. Call "time out" and "foul." Sleep on it if necessary.
15. Use humor and comic relief.
16. Always go for closure.

Useful conflict resolution strategies

Olson and DeFrain cite six basic steps that family therapists and other authorities generally agree on for resolving conflict. The first strategy is to clarify the issue, making sure everyone knows what the conflict is all about. Next, each party must discover what the other party wants or desires. Then, they need to identify various alternatives, brainstorming a wide variety of available options. When the time is right, decide how to negotiate: quid pro quo (this for that) or quid pro quid (this for this). Once the parties have reached an agreement, solidify it (put it in writing if necessary), making sure everyone clearly understands what has been agreed upon, and then review and renegotiate the agreement, as it becomes necessary.

> The first question today's couples ask each other on a date is their credit score.

Don't whitewash red flags!

You may not see a red flag, but have you ever had a gut feeling that something was not quite right? When either a red flag or a gut feeling crops up in a relationship, especially one that precedes marriage, it is a way of telling you that your partner's actions, attitudes, and behaviors have the potential of causing problems. Your partner might have already caused problems, like being untruthful or unfaithful. Other red flags are beliefs or preferences that are very different from your own (religion, jobs, discipline of children, money). Red flags, as in red traffic signals, mean STOP! If you whitewash them during dating and engagement, the whitewash will eventually wear off after you are married, and you will have the very problem you suspected.

To some, a credit score might not matter, but in today's struggling economy, if the person has a poor credit score and a huge amount of debt, it should matter. Does he or she have any friends? (Remember David in Chapter 4, the man who had no friends because he was not willing to be one first?) Does the person have a good history of employment? If it is sketchy, perhaps he or she is looking for a free ride.

Why do people marry the wrong people? Because they start by dating the wrong people for a variety of reasons. They are lonely and insecure (maybe no other man or woman will want to date or marry them). They naively believe the relationship will solve their problems. They think they can change their partner after they get married. They ignore red flags and gut feelings.

Laura married Robert, an alcoholic, because she felt it was her mission in life to cure him of alcoholism. He did not want to stop drinking. Laura lived a life of misery, fighting this demon, but she never left him. She always thought 'maybe today he will change.'

When these ill-matched couples proceed with wedding plans, they have other reasons for not calling the wedding off: 1) It is too late, the invitations have gone out, the flowers have been paid for, the bride has had her final fitting for her dress, and the couple has started to receive gifts. 2) At such a late date, they are embarrassed to admit they are making a mistake. 3) There are many other financial considerations that preclude canceling in the eleventh hour.

If doubts arise about your relationship, check the temperature of your feet. Are the cold? Why? Do you feel that you are settling instead of holding out for a love that is fulfilling? Do you already dislike how your partner treats you privately or in public? Do you really think that your partner will stop abusing you or drinking excessively or cheating on you after the wedding? Are you having second thoughts about him or her making a good spouse? Do you assume that because you have been dating this person for such a long time, you might as well get married? Or, are you the kind of person who thinks that this is your only opportunity to know happiness?

Al was going through a divorce, when he called his about-to-be-ex-wife and told her he had met a young woman. He was afraid that if he didn't propose to her, he would lose her. They had not really dated, but he was the type who didn't want to be alone. That surely should have raised a red flag. In fact, six weeks after a lavish wedding, they split up!

The dreaded "D" word

No couple sets out to get divorced, but statistics make it seem almost inevitable. While the most often cited statistic is 50 percent, the rates actually differ, depending on age, education, and economic status. For college-educated men and women who marry for the first time after the age of twenty-five, the divorce rate is about half of the rate of minority women who do not have a college degree and marry before the age of twenty-five.

The divorce rate in Massachusetts is the lowest in the United States, but that state also happens to have the highest percentage of college graduates.

Some myths and misinformation about divorce might change your perspective on the likelihood that that you too will be divorced one day. Since the 1980s, the divorce rate has been steadily declining, so the more accurate divorce rate ranges between 40 and 50 percent. This

> Women initiate two-thirds of all divorces.

includes people who marry multiple times, thereby increasing the rate. Ten percent of all marriages end in divorce during the first five years and another 10 percent by the tenth year.

Another myth is that cohabitation lowers your chance of divorce. It depends on the circumstances under which you started cohabiting; if it was out of economic necessity, it can reduce your risk of divorce.

Giving marriage another chance increases the chances of another divorce. Approximately 67 to 80 percent of second marriages end in divorce. Third marriages fail at an even higher rate. Divorce evidently does not help us choose better partners but it does teach us how to divorce. (I will not counsel a person who wants to marry for the fourth time.)

Sticker shock might drive some married couples away from divorce court, because they have not learned that getting a divorce need not be expensive. Many states allow couples to get a "do-it-yourself" divorce, which still is heard in a court, but this approach eliminates the long, drawn-out process that can be very contentious and therefore more costly.

Alimony is granted when either the husband or wife is financially dependent on the other. Alimony may be rejected, however, if the wife, qualified and able to find a job commensurate with her husband's job, did not work, or if the couple was not married very long.

The U. S. divorce rate is not the highest compared to other countries. According to the United Nations Demographic Yearbook, the United States has the sixth-highest divorce rate, behind Russia, Belarus, Ukraine, Moldova, and the Cayman Islands, in that order. The lowest rates are in Sri Lanka, Brazil, and Italy, although in those countries, couples may stay together more for religion and financial stability than for love and happiness.

> No one wins or loses in marriage. Both win or both lose.

Hindsight

A survey of divorced people about the disintegration of their marriage resulted in some thoughtful answers that might help others before it is too late, before they have to use hindsight to arrive at the same conclusions.

- Show who you are (faults and all) at the start, because they will come out sooner or later. It's okay to be vulnerable.

- Tell the truth, and you won't have to remember what you said.

- Pay attention to what is happening in your marriage, especially little problems that can become big ones.
- Fight fairly and productively.
- Keep the romance alive in your relationship.
- Talk about sex, learn each other's sexual boundaries, and explore fantasies if it helps to keep your relationship alive. Many partners have strayed to play out their fantasies elsewhere.
- Stay true to yourself.

Points to Ponder

How do complaining and criticizing differ?

What is a soft start-up?

What is a repair attempt? What should you do if your partner offers you one?

What soothing techniques have you used on your partner in an argument? What techniques soothe you most effectively?

What is necessary for compromise to work?

Have you ever initiated a compromise or received an offer of one? How did you react? Did the compromise resolve the argument?

Why should we tolerate another person's faults?

What are Gottman's four horsemen?

Have you ever been in a four horsemen conflict?

How do you react to a gut feeling? Do you pay attention or ignore it? Have you ever ignored one and later regretted it?

How does the body react to disagreements?

What should you do if your body shows physical signs like perspiration or increased breathing during a disagreement?

Would you ever get a divorce? Why? Why not?

12

THE FUEL OF FORGIVENESS

*"A happy marriage is the union
of two good forgivers."*
Ruth Bell Graham

No relationship can live and thrive without the true sense of

forgiveness. Forgiveness is not easy. Very few people know how to

be forgiving. The Church in the New Testament taught us how to forgive, because the source of true happiness lies in the heart of forgiveness. Even if a couple resolves their conflicts, they can remain bitter.

> Forgiveness from the heart must be a part of conflict resolution.

In relationships, we need to learn what needs to be forgiven. Not everything that irritates us or makes us angry needs to be forgiven. Annoying habits are part of everyone's personality. We can be overbearing at times. We can be stubborn at times. But forgiveness is for the person who was disloyal to us or who abandons us. These are the situations that invite thoughts of forgiveness.

Is there anything that should not be forgiven? For human beings, due to our limitations and weaknesses, we might say yes, if someone violates us, rapes us, murders a family member, spouse or child, or if someone abandons us. But if you do not forgive, you remain a hostage forever to the person who violated you. However, talking about forgiveness generates new peace, new hope, and a new future.

In any society, infidelity is a difficult transgression to forgive. A sacred promise has been violated, but if the marriage maintains other strong elements, forgiveness is possible. We are more than sexual beings. People do stupid things, and no wounds are greater than the wounds of the heart. How were you wounded? Was it out of ignorance? Were you wounded out of some kind of slight or annoyance?

I have worked with couples who have faced infidelity. Sometimes the hurt is not just sexual; it could also be by being ignored or not being physically and mentally present. Lying, cheating, and violating someone's interest can also be considered an extramarital affair because the bond between the couple has been broken. It takes a lot of work to mend the break, and most people do not want to invest in the time.

Christ, who taught us numerous times in His ministry on Earth how to forgive or the importance of forgiveness, wants us to forgive those who hurt us and allow healing and new life to come into our marriages.

Here are some forgiveness fundamentals that might help you and your marriage:

- Forgiveness is both a decision and a process. As a decision, it involves using our will and intellect to decide to forgive. We must decide to forgive. As a process, we have to work through the hurt with some caring person who will validate our feelings (a good friend, a priest, a therapist). If you find it difficult to forgive, start with prayer. Ask God for the grace to decide to forgive as you process the hurt.

- Forgiving does not hide the hurt that was done. We have to decide to let go of retribution and allow God to begin the healing in us and in our marriage. By letting go, we open ourselves to redemption and the good that will follow.

- Privately keep a log of your hurts and then destroy the paper as an act of grieving and letting go of the hurts. God will turn our hurts into good when we cede them to Him.

- You are justified in being angry but do not have the right to take your anger out on anyone else. Make time to journal your anger out. One man made a list every day of what person or what situation made him angry. The list changed daily, of course, as he interfaced with different people and encountered situations that spiked his anger. He was able to control his anger by getting them out of his system and onto paper. You own your anger; it does not own you.

- Only God can forgive and forget, but if we say that we do not forget, we are not forgiving.

- Learn to forgive yourself. After you ask forgiveness from God and the person you offended, tell yourself, "I forgive you."

> **Even clean rooms need dusting now and then.**

Risk-taking

It should be easy to tell your marriage partner that they have hurt you, so that you can forgive them, and for them to express their regret. Often it is not that easy. In fact, it is more common to harbor the hurt, to accuse them of inflicting pain on you, to hold your love in abeyance or hold on to resentment that grows into bitterness, even hatred over time. What makes forgiving so difficult? What makes forgiving possible?

In order to be tender and vulnerable with the one you love the most, you take a risk. What if you lose the approval of your beloved? What if you rock an otherwise comfortable boat? What is limiting your courage for producing more joy, love, and fulfillment?

How can you fully love someone when you are holding on to bitterness, sadness or regret? Being vulnerable means both parties are either wounded or blessed.

The following process can give you freedom and support for greater love experiences on all levels of your marriage.

- Make time for your marriage! Use this set-aside time to let the love flow more easily and generously; to honor the love that you share, and to grow your respect for one another. Make sure you will not be interrupted, and take enough time to complete the process of reconnecting in a loving way.

- Recall the depth of love you have for each other, your wedding day, what you love about each other, what brought you together, and how you have grown since you have been married.

- In this same loving context, reflect on any hurts that you have caused your partner or that he or she caused you to feel. Allow each other time to express awareness of these hurts.

- Make a list of things you want to be forgiven for and things you need to forgive:
    - Forgive me for criticizing you for being late.
    - I forgive you for shouting at me when I worked overtime last night.
    - I ask your forgiveness for not listening to your opinion.

- Express appreciation and acknowledgment directly to your loved one for the qualities, strengths, and attributes you most appreciate and love.

Forgiving from the heart offers the forgiver deep inner peace within. It strengthens the mutual connection. In deep peace grows greater love, intimacy, trust, and confidence that help to sustain us through challenging times.

> He that cannot forgive others
> breaks the bridge over which
> he must pass himself; for
> every man has need to be forgiven.
> *Thomas Fuller*

When someone you care about hurts you, you have a choice. You can forgive and move forward or you can hold on to anger, resentment, and thoughts of revenge. (And we know that revenge never ends.)

At some point in our lives, we have been hurt by words or deeds of another. Bullying is the hurt *du jour* these days, but kids have practiced name-calling, snickering, and playing unkind pranks long before bullying became the buzzword.

Our parents may have hurt us unintentionally, or sometimes purposely. Your father snapped at you for not getting better grades, or your mother criticized your choice of husband. In our careers, you can't always escape sabotage of your work or piracy of some creative masterpiece. Even in your marriage, your partner may have had an extramarital affair. It is up to you to decide how you will handle these hurts. Forgiveness can lead you down the path of physical, emotional, and spiritual well-being.

> "In a word, live together in the forgiveness of your sins, for without it no human fellowship, least of all marriage, can survive. Don't insist on your rights, don't blame each other, don't judge or condemn each other, don't find fault with each other, but accept each other as you are, and forgive each other every day from the bottom of your hearts."
> *Dietrich Bonhoeffer*

What is the disadvantage of being unable to forgive?

If you cannot forgive, you are more likely to bring hatred (more than anger) and bitterness into new relationships and experiences. Your life might become so wrapped up in the hurt of having been wronged that you cannot enjoy today. You might become depressed or anxious. You might feel that your life lacks meaning or purpose, or that you have changed your feelings about your spiritual beliefs. You might lose valuable and enriching connectedness with others.

How do I forgive?

Forgiveness doesn't just happen. When someone hurts us or those we love, our first consideration is usually

> ## Forgiveness means letting go.

not forgiveness and mercy. We withdraw, hold negative thoughts, and even consider revenge. Forgiveness is a conscious decision to release resentment and thoughts of revenge. Forgiveness can help you to focus on positive aspects of your life. Forgiveness can even foster feelings of understanding, empathy, and compassion for the one who caused the hurt.

Forgiving the person responsible for hurting you doesn't justify the wrongdoing. You can forgive the person without excusing the act. (A minister's daughter once caused him a lot of grief and heartache by her actions. He said to her, "I love you, but I hate your deed.")

Forgiveness is not about changing the past; it is about changing the future. It allows you to go forward.

What are the benefits of forgiveness?

Releasing bitterness and anger opens the door to compassion, kindness, and peace. Forgiveness can lead to healthier relationships, greater spiritual and psychological well-being, less stress, lower blood pressure, fewer symptoms of depression, and lower risk of alcohol and substance abuse.

Where do I start?

Forgiveness is a commitment to change the way you look at someone or something that caused pain or unhappiness.

- Consider the importance of forgiveness in your life at a given time.
- Remember how you first reacted to the offense and how that reaction has affected your life.
- Make a conscious decision to forgive the offender.
- Take control of your life instead of being a victim. (The person who makes you angry controls you.)

As you release grudges, you will find that they no longer define your life. You might even find compassion and understanding. We have all heard about or read stories of murder and the surviving family member forgiving the killer. These stories are poignant. They teach that forgiveness is possible even in the most painful times in our lives.

Does reconciliation always follow forgiveness?

Reconciliation depends on the relationship of the offender to you. If it is someone you otherwise value, you can reconcile, but not if the offender refuses to communicate or if that person has died. You can still forgive the offender, even if it is not possible to reconcile. It is all about letting go and moving on with your life. Forgiveness is God's commandment; it doesn't mean you cannot trust again.

What if forgiving does not change the one I'm forgiving?

Forgiveness is not about getting the other person to change. Forgiveness is more about how it can change your life by replacing negative thoughts and feelings with peace, happiness, and healing. Forgiveness removes the power from the other person and gives it back to you.

What if I am the one who needs forgiving?

First, you need to honestly assess and acknowledge the wrong you've done and how those wrongs have affected others without judging yourself too harshly. We are human. We make mistakes. You are human, and you will make mistakes. If you are truly remorseful, consider admitting it to those you have hurt. Speak sincerely of your regret and ask for forgiveness without making excuses. You cannot force someone to forgive you; people might not forgive you immediately, but in time, they might realize the sincerity of your apology. Others need to make their own decisions about forgiveness, just as you have had to do. Whatever the outcome, treat others with compassion, empathy, and respect.

Obedience to God's commandments

Forgiveness is a decision we make that is motivated by obedience to God and His command to forgive. The Bible instructs us to forgive as the Lord forgave us:

> "Therefore, as the elect of God, holy and beloved, put on tender mercies, kindness, humility, meekness, longsuffering; bearing with one another, and forgiving one another, if anyone has a complaint against another; even as Christ forgave you, so you also must do." *Colossians 3:12-13*

Since forgiveness goes against human nature, we must forgive by faith, even if we don't feel it. We must trust God to do the work in us that needs to be done so that the forgiveness will be complete.

God honors our commitment to obey Him and our desire to please Him when we choose to forgive. He completes the work in His time.

"Be confident of this very thing, that he which hath begun a good work in you will perform it until the day of Christ Jesus."
Philippians 1:6

Is there any way to know if we have forgiven?

Lewis B. Smedes wrote,

"When you release the wrongdoer from the wrong, you cut a malignant tumor out of your inner life. You set a prisoner free, but you discover that the real prisoner was yourself."

We will know the work of forgiveness is complete when we experience the freedom that comes afterward. We are the ones who suffer most when we choose not to forgive, because we carry around anger, resentment, bitterness, and hurt. Most times, forgiveness is a slow process. Forgiveness releases all that negativity and allows your spirit to soar again.

"Then came Peter to him, and said, Lord, how oft shall my brother sin against me, and I forgive him? Till seven times?'
"Jesus saith unto him, I say not unto thee, until seven times: but until seventy times seven."
Matthew 18:21-22

This answer makes it clear that forgiveness is not an easy thing to accomplish. Often it is not a single event after which we attain a state of forgiveness. It may take a lifetime of forgiving, but we must continue forgiving until the matter is settled in our heart.

Can we still want justice for the one we need to forgive?

It is completely normal to feel anger toward injustice, but only God can judge what is in the heart of another and deal with injustice. We need to release that desire to judge others, because in doing so we release the anger that goes with it.

Why is it important for us to forgive?

Forgiveness is important because it is obedience to the commandment of Jesus. We need to forgive so we will also be forgiven. The New Testament gives us many examples of that commandment.

> "For, if ye forgive men their trespasses, your heavenly Father will also forgive you: But if ye do not forgive men their trespasses, neither will your Father forgive your trespasses." *Matthew 6:14–16*

What forgiveness is and is not

The human brain is amazing. It is like a recording device that tapes all of our experiences, good and bad, happy and sad, pleasant and unpleasant. The human mind is conscious and subconscious. The conscious mind records our present experiences, while the subconscious mind stores our past experiences

> Forgiveness opens the door to the restoration of trust.

(like those memory suitcases we discussed in Chapter 1). Some memories are buried deep and may not be easy to retrieve.

Forgiveness does not rebuild trust or automatically restore it. Trust in marriage is destroyed when one partner is unfaithful. It requires absolute openness if the erring partner claims to have changed. With a consistent pattern of honesty, trust can be restored eventually.

Forgiveness is the only healthy response to an apology. If we decide not to forgive, the barrier remains in place and the relationship is estranged. Time alone does not heal; healing requires the decision to forgive. Forgiveness opens the door to growth. Forgiveness opens the treasures of happiness.

Forgiveness is the fragrance that the
Violet sheds on the heel that has crushed it.
Mark Twain

Points to Ponder

Do you find forgiving easy or difficult?

What attitudes or actions are difficult to forgive? Why?

What, if anything, could you never forgive?

What would you do if your spouse was unfaithful?

Is it possible to forgive and forget?

Do you believe in second chances?

How often should married couples forgive each other?

What things are not necessary to forgive?

Have you ever asked someone to forgive you?

How do you feel when someone forgives you?

Are there things that you can forgive now that you were not able to forgive in the past? What changed?

How do you think forgiveness can make a difference to your health and well-being?

Is it possible to regain trust when it has been violated?

How does forgiveness promote the process of rebuilding trust?

What is God's commandment about forgiveness and how often we should forgive others?

13

ACTS OF LOVE

"Love stretches your heart and makes you big inside."
Margaret Walker

Most busy people keep lists to remind them of things they have to do, either on a daily basis or longer term. There are "To Do" lists, phone number lists, birthday and anniversary lists, grocery lists, long-range planning lists, Internet password lists, and so on. Where would we be without lists?

Although I have already included some smaller lists in this book, I decided to devote this chapter to a list of acts of love we can show our marriage partner. Welcome the habit of doing these positive gestures, and you will do them naturally!

Acts of love

- Express your appreciation. Gottman discovered that happy couples experience twenty positive moments for every negative one in their daily lives. They exchange "a private look," pay a compliment, give an unexpected hug, or tell their partner something positive every day.

One young man had a habit of doing just the opposite. After his wife labored all day to make their home spic and span beautiful and cooked a perfect meal, he would say nothing. He said that only if something was wrong would he say something! Needless to say, that marriage did not last long.

- Express your requests in positive terms and in a calm and peaceful tone. When you start with "I would appreciate it if you would…" or "I would love it if you would…", your requests sound more like favors.

- Be supportive of your spouse. If he or she has had a difficult day at work, give your spouse the opportunity to vent their frustration. Know when to speak and when to remain silent.

- Keep a "third ear" open to your spouse's subtle signals for something he or she wants, like a special meal or a night off to watch a good movie. Silently acknowledge it, and then surprise him or her by fulfilling their wish.

- Set a good example by kicking your own bad habits, especially those pet peeves that you know annoy your spouse.

- Keep a family journal of good times, and periodically read through it to remember those happy times with each other and with good friends.

- Say "I love you" to each other at least once a day or more but not too many times for fear of being misinterpreted as disingenuous.

- Take a walk, play the piano or swim laps to relax when you are angry or upset. It helps you to collect your thoughts.

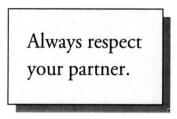

Always respect your partner.

- Show your spouse you can be trusted with whatever he wants to share with you by not passing them along to other family members or friends.

- Do something together every day, even if it is eating breakfast, walking the dog together after dinner, or relaxing to good music.

- Plan activities that you enjoyed sharing when you were dating.

- Tuck love notes in your spouse's briefcase or travel bag whenever he or she goes out of town. Earmark each note with "Do not open until (day of week)" for as long as they will be gone.

- Surprise your spouse with tickets to a game with his favorite sports team or a concert with her favorite performer. Enter into their enjoyment and excitement.

- Find creative ways to let go of pet peeves. One woman entered a newspaper contest for the longest list of a spouse's pet peeves. She ended up submitting the longest list (125) to the columnist.

- You cannot change your spouse. Period.

- Make a conscious effort to put each other first, and you will have a win-win proposition.

- Send flowers for no occasion, just because you love her or him.

- Be a good receiver. Delight over gifts, inexpensive or costly, from your spouse.

- If your spouse is facing a tight deadline at work, offer to help. (One woman worked a full schedule but often went to her workaholic husband's office and typed for him until the wee hours of the next morning. As it turned out, they made a great business team!)

- Reveal something new and endearing about yourself every now and then. It triggers an "I didn't know that" from your spouse and engenders a good feeling.

- Use affirmative words to speak deeply of your love. Examples: "You make my day." "What would I do without you?"

- Spend quality time with one another; turn off the TV, and give undivided attention to conversation.

14

EMBRACING ENDURANCE

*"If I had to tell you how much you mean,
I would never get a chance to finish."*
Anonymous

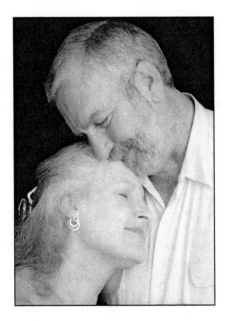

Have you ever seen a photograph in the newspaper of an elderly couple celebrating their 75th wedding anniversary? Did you notice a sparkle in their eyes or how they tweaked each other's nose? Did you observe how their smiles at each other seem to have a special meaning? Do they finish each other's punch lines to jokes? They look as much in love as when they married so many years earlier. Surely they faced life's problems such as disease or other health problems, death of loved ones, financial crises, yet their love triumphed.

John and Ann Betar, 101 and 97 respectively and both Syrian, recently celebrated the honor of being named the "longest married couple" in the United States. They were married for eighty years. They eloped to escape an arranged marriage by her father. The happily married couple, after all these years with five children, fourteen grandchildren, and sixteen great grandchildren, has no secrets to a long and happy marriage, but they do have a few rules: 1) live with contentment, 2) live within your means, and 3) go with the flow.

The happiest people don't necessarily have the best of everything; they just make the most of everything they have. John and Ann Betar are a shining example of this truism.

The state motto of Michigan is "If you seek a pleasant peninsula, look about you." If you seek a successful marriage, look at others, how they relate to each other, how they look lovingly at each other, and how they take care of each other.

In a New York Times article published on December 23, 2012, three sisters and their spouses, each wed for thirty-two years, discussed how they have made their marriages last. One sister, Susan, said, "We give each other space to do our own thing." Another sister, Carol, echoed advice from their mother, "You better like him because he's not going to change." The third sister, Beth, attributed acceptance as her key to making marriage last. "We accept each other and grow with each other. Sailing [their common interest] has been part of the glue that has kept us together."

The spouses had their own reasons for making their marriage last. One said, "First, you have to like your wife. And I like her a lot. I love her. That's a good foundation. Next, we don't get overexcited about any difference of opinion. We just deal with it. Last, we don't expect perfection from each other or a perfect marriage." The second spouse, married to Carol, said, "Our marriage is like being on a team. Carol does the finances. I do the shopping." Sam, who is Beth's spouse, summed up their reasons with his own contribution. "I think you can't get angry and you have to listen. You always have to be kind. We spend our free time together."

In one marriage, the husband had been diagnosed with a rare type of cancer and received little chance of survival. When this crisis hit the family, he didn't roll over and give into his disease. He continued to live according to his normal routines. No matter how chemo affected him or how he looked, he went to work and did his regular work-outs at the gym. Another spouse recently received word that he has to have brain surgery to remove a tumor. His wife says that they will take the challenge one step at a time. "We are each other's best friend."

Empty-nesting

Empty-nesting is where the couple, now married thirty years or more, realizes that there are no more buffers, no more children to distract, no more homework to do, no more activities to give excuses for not doing some task. When they reflect on these things, they can renew their married life as an eagle renews its feathers. It is a wonderful sort of loving relationship, because now they can be more open to each other, take their time and not rush with whatever they choose to do, and even talk in a new language. Their hearts are softened, their mood has mellowed, and they become kinder people.

The "empty-nest" season of a marriage can feel like a second honeymoon. Many couples welcome their new freedom, while others have a hard time letting go of the hustle and bustle of raising a family. And sometimes that new freedom does not last.

In the empty-nest stage suddenly a retired couple might find a son or daughter who needs a temporary home, financial assistance during hard times, or perhaps babysitting duties of the grandkids.

If their children are grown and gone and not needing their parents, empty-nest couples can experience satisfaction. Because there are no children, the mother has less work to do at home or may be retired from her own career outside the home, and the father may be retired too. The relationship can take a leap for better or for worse. The later years can also bring major health issues and the gradual loss of abilities.

Empty-nesters face the possibility of one spouse preceding the other in death. The surviving partner goes through a period of adjustment, similar to one that a divorced partner experiences. Divorce and death bring separation, although the dynamics of the two are dissimilar.

Men and women who marry after a divorce or death of a spouse or after waiting for the right person experience in their later years some of the same adjustments of young married couples. Sometimes they latch on to someone who reminds them of their dearly departed spouse. They may find comfort in their choice, but sometimes they regret it. For them, too, I believe the waiting period before dating should be one to two years.

How did they do it?

Couples that have weathered all of the storms of married life and did it with honesty and integrity enjoy the golden years with renewed interest in their marriage. But how did they manage to come this far in a nation of disposable marriages?

In the first place, if they committed to stay with their marriage, work out their problems, love and forgive one another, and practice their faith together, they upheld the true meaning of their covenant.

They lived by the highest standards of conduct, honoring their oath to be loyal and faithful to each other. Their marriage was built on a strong foundation of respect and love and fidelity, as Christ expected of them.

The senior marriage partners maintained dignity and grace under pressure. Who knows how many difficulties, trials and tribulations they faced in fifty or more years of marriage, putting them under a great deal of pressure? They learned to balance their emotions during these times, using their intelligence and serenity.

They keep the door of honest communication open, making the perspective on issues larger and inclusive. They learned to transform insignificant situations into memorable times of pleasure. They took delight in ordinary life, appreciating what they have instead of trying to keep up with their neighbors.

At the end of a long and happy marriage, they realize that divorce was never an option; they had made a lifelong commitment, a covenant. They had known that neither one was perfect, but with patience, they accepted each other, faults and all. They practiced give-and-take in their love for one another, each going more than halfway.

These couples live each day to the fullest and even continue dating as if they never got married. They keep the romance alive, despite the many ups and downs they have faced throughout their marriage. Through honest communication, they are able to diffuse disagreements that might have grown to more serious arguments or conflicts; they have learned the value of choosing their words carefully.

How do couples take into account their new freedom, increased time together, possibly decreased income, and fading health and energy? Some do it with grace and style, because over the years they have learned flexibility and tolerance. Some have always been active, so that with more freedom they can do more volunteer work or mentoring to the younger generations. They join groups or organizations for people in their peer group, travel together, or take up new hobbies. Moreover, this is a time for them to deepen their spiritual life in preparation for physical limitations or losses that will surely come later.

Points to Ponder

1. How has your love grown over the years?

2. In what ways did your marriage improve since you first got married?

3. Do you feel as much in love as you did when you first got married? More? Less?

4. What are the most important ingredients needed to sustain a long and happy marriage?

5. As a couple, how have you handled the difficulties you have faced in your marriage such as illness, financial setbacks, even death? Have these challenges made you a stronger couple? If so, how?

6. How did your marriage change after you became empty-nesters?

7. In what ways do you utilize the freedom you have without children at home?

8. What advice would you give to a young couple just starting their married life?

"There is nothing that can replace the absence of someone dear to us, and one should not even attempt to do so. One must simply hold out and endure it. At first that sounds very hard, but at the same time it is also a great comfort. For the extent the emptiness truly remains unfilled one remains connected to the other person through it. It is wrong to say that God fills the emptiness. God in no way fills it but much more leaves it precisely unfilled and thus helps us preserve—even in pain—the authentic relationship. Furthermore, the more beautiful and full the remembrance, the more difficult the separation. But gratitude transforms the torment of memory into silent joy. One bears what was lovely in the past not as a thorn but as a precious gift deep within, a hidden treasure of which one can always be certain."

Dietrich Bonhoeffer

RESOURCES BY CHAPTER

Chapter 1
Adler, Alfred. Birth order and personality. www.adlerian.us

Hartshone, Joshua K. "How Birth Order Affects Your Personality." Scientific American (online). January 11, 2010.

Kahlil Gibran, The Prophet.

St. John Chrysostom, "On Marriage and Family Life."

St John Chrysostom, Homily 20 on Ephesians.

Proverbs 22:6 King James Version

Walcutt, Diana L. PhD. "Birth Order & Personality."
http://psychcentral.com

www.birthorderpersonality.com

Chapter 2
"Everything You Wanted to Know about Puberty."
www.kidshealth.org

Freud, Sigmund. On Sexuality. Penguin Books, 1991, p. 67.

Ware, Bishop Kallistos. ""The Sacrament of Love: The Orthodox Understanding of Marriage and its Breakdown," *The Downside Review*, 109, no. 375 (April 1991), 79-93

"Puberty and Adolescence." National Institute of Health. www.nlm.nih.gov

Puppy love. http://opinion.inquirer.net

Short, Ray E. "Sex, Love and Romance." 2004.

Chapter 3
Aristotle. "What Would Aristotle Say About Friendship?"

Ephesians 5:25 King James Version
1 Corinthians 13:11 King James Version

St John Chrysostom, Homily 20 on Ephesians.

Fromm, Erich. The Art of Loving.

How to Love Yourself in 17 Ways. abundancetapestry.com

Wadell, Paul J. Happiness & the Christian Moral Life. Rowman & Littlefield Publishing, Inc. 2012

www.getyourowndirt.com

Chapter 4
Aristotle. "What Would Aristotle Say about Friendship?"

Gottman, John M. and Nan Silver. The Seven Principles for Making Marriage Work. New York: Three Rivers Press, 1999.

Precious Vessels of the Holy Spirit. Protecting Veil Press, p. 177.

2 Peter 1:5 King James Version

"The Value of Friends and Friendship." Voices.yahoo.com

Wadell, Paul. Happiness & the Christian Moral Life.

Chapter 5
Atik, Chiara. The New York Times (2011) article on women delaying marriage. Posted in HowAboutWe.

Archimandrite Aimilianos of Simonopetra. "Marriage: The Great Sacrament." orthodoxinfo.com/praxis/marriage.aspx

Ephesians 5:8 King James Version

Ephesians 5: 21-22 King James Version

1 Corinthians 7:27-28 King James Version

1 Corinthians 13:4-8 King James Version

1 John 4:8 King James Version

Milford, Anne and Jennifer Gauvain. How Not to Marry the Wrong Guy: A Guide for Avoiding the Biggest Mistake of Your Life.

Nestor, Theo Pauline. "Is He the Wrong Man for You?"

Romans 5:7-8 King James Version

Romans 8:26 King James Version

Tessina, Tina B. PhD. "Money, Sex & Kids – Stop Fighting about Three Things That Can Ruin Your Relationship."

The Wedding Report.com

Titus 3:3 King James Version

Wadell, Paul. Happiness & the Christian Moral Life.

Chapter 6
Ephesians 5:25 King James Version

1 Corinthians 11:11-12 King James Version

Archimandrite Aimilianos of Simonopetra. "Marriage: The Great Sacrament." orthodoxinfo.com/praxis/marriage.aspx

Gottman, John M. and Nan Silver. Seven Principles for Making Marriage Work.

Harris, Victor W. MS. Preparing for Marriage: 10 Things You'll Wish You Knew

Peterson, Ann. "Preparing for Marriage While Planning a Wedding."

U. S. Bureau of Census, 2003-2004

Wadell, Paul. Happiness & the Christian Moral Life

Chapter 7
Elements of a Covenant Relationship. covanantmarriage.com

1 Corinthians 13:8 King James Version

Hosea 2:19 King James Version

Truths of a Covenant of Marriage. Covenantmarriage.com

20 Tips for Writing Your Own Vows

Wadell, Paul. Happiness & the Christian Moral Life

Wedding Vows and Readings. wedding.theknot.com

Chapter 8
Hanks, Julie, LCSW. "Empathy: The Secret Sauce to a Happy Marriage." RealAge.com. July 9, 2012.

Otremba, Maureen, MA and James Otremba, M.Div, MS. "Newly Married" foryourmarriage.org

"The Newlywed's Guide to a Happy Marriage." The Reader's Digest, 2012.

The Orthodox Christian Marriage. "Characteristics of a Successful Marriage."

Time, Sex and Money. A research study conducted by Creighton University, 2000, cited in "Newly Married." foryourmarriage.org

3 Steps to a Great Marriage: Be Friends & Lovers. Aish.com

Wayne State University Study – Establishing Relationships with Other Newlyweds Strengthens Young Married Couples' Relationship. Detroit, Michigan

Young, Cheryl. "Creating Successful Foundations in Your Marriage (or any Relationship). creativeblueprints.com

Chapter 9
Hannon, Kerry. Money and Marriage. Forbes. July 4, 2012.

Hebrews 13:5 King James Version

Ramsey, Dave. Newlyweds: What Do We Need to Know about Money? Daveramsey.com

Ramsey, Dave. The Truth about Money and Relationships. Daveramsey.com

Chapter 10
Dyer, Wayne. You'll See It When You Believe It. New York: William Morrow, 2001.

Hemingway, Ernest.

Hiemstra, Kristin. "How to Have Grace under Pressure." The Art of Potential. May 7, 2012. chapelboro.com

Philippians 4:13 King James Version

Chapter 11

"The Divorce Experience: A Study of Divorce at Midlife and Beyond." AARP Magazine online. 2008.

Ephesians 4:26 King James Version

1 Corinthians 9:24 King James Version

Gottman, John and Nan Silver. Seven Principles of Making Marriage Work.

Olson, David H. and John DeFrain. Marriage and the Family. Mayfield Publishing Company, 1997.

2 Timothy 4:7 King James Version

Shapiro, Dana Adam. You Can Be Right (or You Can Be Married), Scribner, 2012.

Chapter 12

Chapman, Gary. Things I Wish I'd Known before We Got Married.

Colossians 3:13 King James Version

Fairchild, Mary. "What Does the Bible Say about Forgiveness?" christianity.about.com

"Forgiveness: Letting Go of Grudges and Bitterness." mayoclinic.com/health/forgiveness

Father Pio, quoted in "Forgiveness Fundamentals" by Maureen Otremba MA and James Otremba, M.Div, MS foryourmarriage.org

Gottman, John M. and Nan Silver. The Seven Principles for Making Marriage Work.

Matthew 6:14-16 King James Version

Matthew 18:21-22 King James Version

Otrema, Maureen MA and James Otremba, M.Div, MS "Forgiveness Fundamentals." foryourmarriage.org

Philippians 1:6 King James Version

Smedes, Lewis B. Forgive and Forget: Healing the Hurts We Don't Deserve. HarperOne. 2007

Taylor, Anne. "How Forgiveness in Marriage Builds Intimacy." huffingtonpost.com

Chapter 13

"Be Equally Committed." Study cited in Journal of Psychological Science. 2011.

"Double Date" – Wayne State University study, 2010.

Epstein, Robert PhD "Let Love Build." Quoted in "10 Things Happy Couples Do."

Gottman, John M. and Nan Silver. The Seven Principles for Making Marriage Work.

Lay, Rachael. "Creating Good Love Habits."

Penner, David PhD. "Accentuate the Positive." Quoted in "10 Things Happy Couples Do"

Rosenblatt, Paul PhD. "Do This in Bed" from Two in a Bed: The Social System of Couple Bed Sharing.

"Skip Small Talk." Study cited in Journal of Psychological Science. 2010.

Chapter 14

FoxNews.com

"Later Years" foryourmarriage.org

How beautiful, then, the marriage of two Christians,
Two who are one in hope, one in desire,
One in the way of life they follow,
One in the religion they practice...
Nothing divides them,
Either in flesh or in spirit.
They are, in very truth, two in one flesh;
And where there is but one flesh there is also but one spirit.
They pray together, they worship together,
They fast together; instructing one another,
Encouraging one another, strengthening one another...
They have no secrets from one another;
They never shun each other's company;
They never bring sorrow to each other's heart.

Tertullian, To his wife, ACW 13

PHOTO CREDITS

CPSIA information can be obtained at www.ICGtesting.com
Printed in the USA
BVOW08s0029080813

327808BV00002B/5/P